Understanding the Medical Diagnosis of Child Maltreatment:

A Guide for NonMedical Professionals

Prepared by:
Jean C. Smith, M.D., Rebecca L. Benton, M.D., M.P.H.
Joyce K. Moore, R.N., M.P.H., Desmond K. Runyan, M.D., Dr.P.H.
University of North Carolina – Chapel Hill Department of Pediatrics

Supported by:
North Carolina Department of Human Resources
Division of Social Services
Child Protective Services Unit

ISBN 0-930915-02-X

Published by:
American Humane Association
63 Inverness Drive East
Englewood, CO 80112-5117
303-792-9900

FOREWARD

The American Humane Association is committed to providing the best information available to caseworkers, professionals, and parents involved with the tremendous challenges of protecting children. It is imperative that Child Protective Services workers and others dealing with these complicated issues have all the information and resources they need in order to make informed and effective decisions regarding the abuse and/or neglect of children.

Caseworkers must possess a familiarity with medical terminology and its usage to assist them in diagnosing suspected child abuse and/or neglect. Such knowledge allows for informed and reliable communication between the caseworker, who is responsible for protecting a child from further harm, and the physician who is evaluating the child for medical diagnosis and treatment.

For over a decade, this publication has been a valuable resource to the child welfare field. It provides a basic, understandable approach to information on diagnosing suspected abuse and/or neglect in a reader-friendly format. This revised edition offers expanded information in a number of areas, especially in the area on child sexual abuse, and includes new illustrations and diagrams.

Originally prepared for the North Carolina Department of Human Resources, this material continues to be a useful resource to child protective workers nationwide. It is with continued appreciation to the North Carolina Department of Human Resources, Division of Social Services, Child Protection Unit, and to the authors for their diligence in seeing that the information contained herein is up-to-date and accurate, that we are pleased to present this revised edition of *Understanding the Medical Diagnosis of Child Maltreatment: A Guide for Nonmedical Professionals.*

Karen J. Farestad, Ph.D.
Director, Children's Division
American Humane Association

TABLE OF CONTENTS

INTRODUCTION

This manual was composed primarily for North Carolina Protective Service workers investigating cases of alleged child abuse and neglect. Funding was received from the North Carolina Department of Human Resources. The manual was prepared by professionals working with the Child Medical Evaluation Program, located in The Department of Pediatrics at The University of North Carolina at Chapel Hill.

The work in this manual is intended to convey current medical viewpoints regarding child maltreatment. If any recommendations made regarding the role of the Protective Service worker in case investigation and management are in conflict with current state policy, the worker should adhere to state policy.

The purpose of this manual is to facilitate communication between Child Protective Service workers and medical practitioners. This text provides nonmedical professionals with explanations of the medical terminology, techniques and diagnoses frequently utilized in the physician's report. It provides guidelines for social workers in their determinations to seek medical examinations in a timely fashion. It is hoped that this information will contribute to the CPS worker's understanding of the physician's report and will also aid in the task of helping families understand and carry through with follow-up care for children. Our purpose is to make the CPS worker's job easier, by providing a desk-top reference of easily accessible answers to frequently asked questions concerning the medical aspects of child abuse and neglect.

If one examines retrospectively each professional involved in a case of abuse, it becomes apparent that the CPS worker carries not only the most burden, but also the most gratification in this process. He or she has access to information from every aspect of the case, as well as coordination of the social, medical, and legal information needed to resolve it. However, what appears in writing to be a simple process between the three concerned parties often becomes a process confused by jargon, roles, and misdirected information.

It should not be interpreted that the CPS worker's job is solely to relay information between these three sources, but rather to provide a framework for communication among all of these sources. It is most important that the worker's own relationships with each be as succinct and as clear as possible. In this manual, we hope to clarify the maintenance of communication between the social worker and medical practitioner.

From our interviews with social workers and physicians, we have found varied problems in the connections between these two. Interaction with physicians can be intimidating to the social worker. We hope to give you information that will enhance your professional knowledge base so that you can effectively communicate with physicians. It is important to understand medical terminology and information so that your referrals can be concise and elicit information from the report to develop an effective plan for the child. Clearly voiced concern and follow-up to the physician with needed information and results can create a professional atmosphere that we all desire.

With this manual, you, the CPS worker, have the tools to better understand and confer with the physicians who offer medical opinions in your cases. Do not be afraid to ask specific questions or to request explanations, no matter how trivial they may seem. Remember, the role of the physician is to help *you* in your assessment of the case; use him or her to the best of your ability, for their experience and knowledge can be one of your most important resources in providing a safe and secure plan for a child.   ....(1989)

PREFACE TO CURRENT REVISION

During the seven years since its first printing, the manual has been used in training hundreds of Child Protective Service workers for the North Carolina Division of Social Services. Although the manual was primarily written for use by the CPS worker, it has also been used by attorneys, law enforcement, juvenile judges, and other nonmedical professionals for training and reference.

In this present revision, we have added new research findings and information in the areas of head injury, radiographic findings, parental substance abuse, and sexual abuse. We have also attempted to respond to the feedback from workshop participants. We are most pleased to have added the expertise of special contributors to this edition - Dr. Gail Brown, Medical Director of the North Carolina State Child Fatality Prevention Team; and Dr. John Butts, North Carolina Chief Medical Examiner, for the section "Child Abuse Fatalities: The Role of the Medical Examiner."

We also thank Alexia Keller-Gussman for the literature search and Julia Norem-Coker for organizing the literature and her efforts to find and direct Frank Li's excellent illustrations for this edition.

Rebecca Benton's extensive contribution to the first edition deserves special note. As a graduate English major, Becky assisted with writing the original manual and assured that medical terminology was well "translated" for the nonmedical professional. Since that time, she has received her Masters of Public Health, completed UNC Medical School, and is currently an intern in Pediatrics. The proofreading by Janet Clegg and editing and manuscript preparation by Christine Curtis were invaluable.

Most importantly, we wish to thank the North Carolina Department of Human Resources for the funding and support of both the original manual and this revision.

Jean C. Smith, M.D.
Joyce K. Moore, R.N., M.P.H
(1997)

PHYSICAL ABUSE

The Cutaneous Manifestations of Abuse

Cutaneous manifestations of abuse are injuries such as bruises and abrasions which pertain to the skin. Recognizing and interpreting their significance is one of the most frequently utilized skills of the Protective Service worker. Remember, however, that you are not alone in determining the nature of these injuries. The physician will play a crucial role in helping distinguish abuse from differential skin conditions, diseases, or accidental trauma. All children sustain some bruises and scratches in their normal, everyday play. In your attempts to distinguish these "play" injuries from abusive ones, it is *crucial* that you obtain a very detailed, concise history. In relating this history to the doctor, be sure to include details such as how long ago the incident occurred, and the exact details of the accident. For example, how tall was the table from which he fell, or what he was playing when he bruised his legs or buttocks? In determining the etiology of cutaneous injuries, the doctor must look at several aspects of the child's condition, such as the ages of the various bruises and abrasions and their specific location, shape, and size.

I. Dating Bruises

Bruising occurs when some force disrupts the small vessels under the skin, allowing blood to escape. Bleeding usually starts immediately following the injury and may continue briefly, or for hours, depending on the force of the injury, the size of the damaged vessels, the type of tissue injured, and the adequacy of the victim's coagulation mechanism (the body's ability to stop bleeding by itself). For a child who has no coagulation deficiencies or blood disorders, use the following general guidelines in assessing the bruise.

A. Where is the bruise?

Loose skin with vessels unsupported by underlying bony or muscular structures will bruise more easily than supported skin. This makes the eyelids and genitalia predisposed to bruising following even minor trauma. Sometimes the injured vessels are located so deeply under the skin that it takes days for the blood to migrate to the surface and become visible. These deep-seated bruises may remain dark for days or weeks.

B. What color is the bruise?

Once the bleeding has stopped, the body begins to break down the blood into products which can be absorbed by surrounding tissue. *Hemoglobin*, one of the constituents of the blood, changes colors in a sequential fashion as it breaks down. It is possible to estimate the age of the bruise from the color that the hemoglobin in the injury has assumed.

The following chart was adapted from Drs. Spitz and Fisher (1926).

Color	Time of photograph
Light bluish-red	After a few hours
Purple (dark)	Within one week
Green-yellow	End of one week
Brown	Later than one week
Disappearance	Two to four weeks

C. What size is the bruise?

The color of the bruise begins to fade from the edges inward, causing the bruise to get smaller and smaller as it begins to heal. If the size of the bruise is no longer compatible with the size of the force which caused it, then the bruise is most likely old enough to have started healing.

D. Documentation

It is essential that either you or the physician carefully document the bruises with color photographs or slides. (Polaroids are not as clear nor detailed, but are certainly better than nothing at all.) The pictures should be taken early within the first few days of the incident. Be sure that they clearly show the locations, size, and color of the injury. Keep in mind that the bruises may not appear on the skin until a few days after the trauma; thus, the photos taken on the same day of the incident may not show the true extent of the injury. If you have access to the child, try to take another set of photos a few days after the first set. The changes in color at this stage may greatly enhance the credibility of your evidence. Do not assume that the physician's documentation will always be adequate. Taking the time to rephotograph the child may provide crucial evidence for your case. If you and the physician lack experience or expertise with photography, you may find it useful to contact the local police department for an experienced photographer.

II. Common sites of bruises – Accident vs. Abuse

The actual location of the bruise is helpful not only in determining its age, but also in differentiating an abusive contusion from one that is accidental, a "play bruise." Bruises occurring over the bony prominences, such as the knees, shins, forehead, or elbows, are more likely to be accidental than those occurring over areas of soft tissue, such as the cheeks, buttocks, or stomach. Most falls produce one bruise on a single surface, while abusive bruises frequently cover many areas of the body.

A. Face and head

Accidental bruises usually occur over the bony prominences, such as the forehead or chin. It is not uncommon for babies in the first few months of life to scratch their cheeks, ears, nose, and eyes with their fingernails, which are often long and hard to cut. Bruises of the forehead are not uncommon on the child who is just learning to walk and climb. Injuries to the soft tissue of the cheeks may be due to slapping or pinching.

B. Upper lip and frenulum

Bruises or lacerations inside the mouth in these areas usually come from having a bottle or feeding spoon jammed into the baby's mouth. These types of injuries cannot be self-inflicted until the baby is old enough to sit up and fall forward. They are often accompanied by a history of inconsolable crying. (See "Oral Trauma" in the section, "Injuries to the Head, Eyes, Ears, Nose, and Mouth.")

C. Ear

Pinch marks on the earlobe are not uncommon, as is swelling of the external ear, caused from blows to that tissue. Repetitive injury will cause a characteristic "cauliflower ear." Children who have been pinched or pulled on the earlobe usually have a matching mark on each surface.

D. Neck

Any strange bruises or cuts on the neck are almost always due to being choked or strangled by a human hand, rope, dog collar, etc. Similar marks may come from sudden traction on a shirt or bib.

E. Knee or shin

These are the most common sites for accidental bruises, not only in the child who is learning to walk, but also in older children, who may fall when playing, or bump into objects.

F. Buttocks, lower back, and lateral thighs

Almost always related to punishment from paddling, multiple bruises of this area are not commonly accidental.

G. Genitals, inner thighs

Pinch marks, cuts, and abrasions are sometimes found on the penis, frequently related to punishment in toilet training. Deep grooves on the penis may be inflicted tying off the penis with a rubber band or string. Multiple bruises of this area are not usually accidental. Parents or guardians of children with accidental genital injuries will usually give a specific, detailed, unsolicited history, for example, "the zipper caught his scrotum." Because of the tenderness of the area and its tendency to bleed profusely, both the parents/caretakers and children are immediately aware of these injuries; children sustaining accidental genital trauma are usually brought immediately to the emergency room. Sexual abuse should also be considered when injuries are present in this area. In these cases, the physician may check for other signals of sexual abuse, such as the presence of sexually transmitted diseases.

III. Common patterns of abuse

A. "Loop" marks

One of the most commonly recognized abusive marks is a characteristic "loop" mark made from a flexible object such as a belt, electric cord or clothesline. Multiple bruises or lesions of this type are *pathognomonic* (indicative) of abuse. There are no naturally occurring illnesses which cause this type of mark. (See Figure 1)

Figure 1

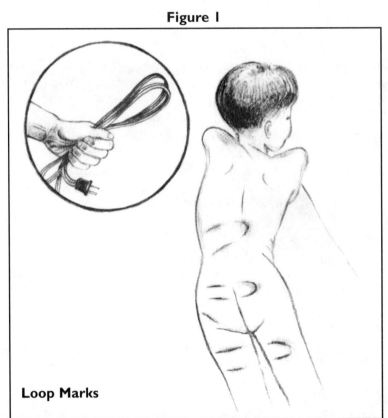

Loop Marks

B. Hand marks

1. Grab marks or fingertip bruises

This common manifestation of abuse is notable by the characteristic oval-shaped bruises resembling fingertips. Often these bruises are inflicted on children who are violently shaken. Other symptoms of the "whiplash shaken infant syndrome" will most likely help support this theory. (See "The Whiplash Shaken Infant Syndrome" in the section,

"Injuries to the Head, Eyes, Ears, Nose, and Mouth.") The most common sites for these marks are on the upper arm, shoulder, and the extremities of children who cannot yet walk.

Sometimes a parent/caretaker will squeeze a child's cheeks in order to force food or medicine into the mouth. This action characteristically leaves a thumb mark on one cheek with several finger-tip marks on the other.

2. Encirclement bruises

These bruises occur when a child is grabbed around the chest or stomach. The characteristic pattern is one or two thumb prints on one side of the body, with as many as eight finger marks on the other.

3. Slap marks

Slap marks frequently leave two or three linear, parallel bruises similar to the outline of the fingers. (See Figure 2)

Figure 2

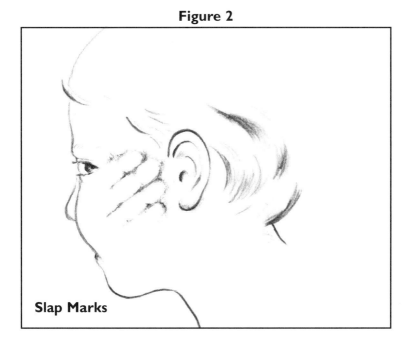

Slap Marks

C. Bite marks

Bite marks produce pairs of elliptical, crescent-shaped bruises or lacerations, often containing individual teeth marks. Sometimes the two crescents meet to form a complete circle. Bite marks inflicted during sexual intercourse may have a central area of bruising, a "suck mark," or a "thrust mark."

The most common areas where bites occur are the limbs, abdomen, and cheeks. Frequently a forensic odontologist or forensic pathologist may be able to match the pattern of the bite to a mold of the perpetrator's teeth. Therefore, it is important that these contusions be well documented with photographs and diagrams.

D. Gag marks

A child whose mouth has been gagged will usually have bruises extending from the corners of the mouth.

E. Circumferential marks

Circumferential tie marks around the ankles and/or wrists can be caused when a child is tied up. Depending on the material used, these marks are often in the form of rope burns or other friction burns, appearing as a large blister that circles the entire extremity. If the child has been tied to another object, the abrasions will only cover part of the ankle or wrist.

F. Strap marks

Strap marks are usually one to two inches wide and linear. In those caused by a belt, the eyelets or buckle can sometimes be discerned. Lash marks are thinner than strap marks. In both, the distal end of the strap usually hits the hardest, sometimes breaking the skin and leaving a loop-shaped mark. Long, linear scratches or bruises are often caused by switches such as tree branches.

G. Marks caused by other objects

Bizarre bruises with sharply defined borders are almost always inflicted. Often the object can be identified by the shape of the contusion. For example, a hairbrush would leave many small puncture wounds, while a comb may leave many small linear bruises from being dragged across the skin.

H. Hair loss

Alopecia, or loss of hair, can signal several different problems in a child's condition. Parents or caretakers who use a child's hair as a convenient handle for seizing him or her will pull out patches of hair. This injury can be especially dangerous when it causes a *subgaleal hematoma*, a separation between the scalp and the skull which fills with blood. (See description and figure in "Injuries to the Head, Eyes, Ears, Nose, and Mouth.")

Differential

- *Trichotillomania*, a psychological condition in which the child pulls out his own hair, may be confused with abuse, and requires psychological treatment.
- *Tinea Capitis* (ringworm) is a fungus which may cause circular patches of hair to fall out.
- Various nutritional deficiencies can cause the hair to fall out.
- *Idiopathic* hair loss has no apparent cause. This is always a possibility when no other abusive symptoms exist. In this condition, the scalp is smooth and hair follicles are very sparse or absent.

IV. Neglect

A neglected child can often be identified by skin which is dirty and uncared for. Severe, untreated diaper rash; feces in the folds of skin and under the nails; or multiple insect, rat, or dog bites; when severe and prolonged, *might* be indicators of neglect, if the parent refuses to respond to help and education. In failure to thrive, the infant's skin seems "baggy" and loose, since underlying muscle tissue and fat have been used by the body for energy. Loss of hair may also be seen in failure to thrive. Children with an excessive amount of "play" bruises which are not attributed to a bleeding disorder may also be victims of neglect through lack of supervision.

V. Differentials - Bleeding disorders, dermatological disorders, naturally occurring marks, and folk practices

A. Bleeding disorders

In his assessment for abuse or neglect, the physician will consider if the child has certain bleeding disorders which make him or her predisposed to bruising. A child whose blood does not coagulate properly will have an abnormal amount of blood released from injured vessels. This not only means that the child will bleed more profusely from an open wound, but that he or she will also bleed more profusely under the skin, causing it to appear more bruised than it normally would. Examples of bleeding disorders are:

1. Hemophilia
An inherited disease in which blood fails to clot adequately and abnormal bleeding occurs.

2. Leukemia
A disease in which there is a tremendous increase in the number of immature white blood cells which are unable to fight infection. There is also a

---

marked decrease in the production of platelets and red blood cells, causing a child to "bruise easily." What otherwise might be a relatively mild infection may prove fatal for someone with leukemia.

3. Idiopathic Thrombocytopenic Purpura (ITP)
A bleeding disorder characterized by a marked decrease in the number of blood platelets in the system, resulting in multiple bruises.

4. Lack or malabsorption of fat soluble vitamins, particularly vitamin K.

The frequent allegation that a child simply "bruises easily" can be tested legitimately by medical tests for this condition. It is important to remember, however, that bleeding disorders and abuse are not mutually exclusive; children with these medical conditions are just as likely to be abused as other children. Most likely, the physician will perform a bleeding function test for these disorders. Some of the most common tests are prothrombin (PT), partial thromboplastin (PTT), and bleeding time.

Other causes of abnormal bleeding are viral infections which can sometimes produce anticoagulants which circulate in the blood and cause the child to bleed or bruise easily. There are also some medications which cause coagulation problems in children. One common drug is *salicylate*, or aspirin, which a parent or caretaker may add to a baby's bottle to relieve pain. Too much of this or similar drugs can cause a child to bruise easily. The physician will usually request a list of any medications which the child may be taking at that time.

B. Dermatological disorders

1. Ehlers-Danlos syndrome
This is an inherited disorder of collagen fibers, in which the skin is velvety, hyperelastic, and fragile. Minor trauma may lead to bruises, hematomas, poor healing, and wide shiny "paper-thin" scars. Bleeding studies are normal.

2. Allergic skin conditions
Skin conditions such as *erythema multiforme* (unexplained red blotches that turn into bruises; rash progresses if child is kept under observation) and *uticaria pigmentosa* (darkened area on the skin which erupts into "hives" when rubbed or irritated) are thought to have an allergic process.

3. Phytodermatitis
This is a reaction to a phototoxin, which occurs when the skin is touched by the juice of certain plants and then exposed to the sun. Plants that may produce this include lime, lemon, fig, parsnip, celery, and herbal preparations.

4. Contact dermatitis
Contact dermatitis can be caused by exposure to detergents, rubber substances, poison ivy, etc.

C. Naturally occurring cutaneous marks confused with abuse

1. Mongolian spots
Appearing as grayish blue, clearly defined spots on the buttocks, back, legs, upper arms, and shoulders, these birthmarks are those most commonly mistaken for abuse. They are present at birth and usually last from two to three years, but can persist into adulthood. In a recent study, Mongolian spots were present in 10% of the Caucasian babies examined, 95% of the African-American babies, 80% of the Asiatics, and 70% of the Hispanic and Native Americans.

2. Maculae cerulae
These bluish spots appear on the skin concomitantly with head or pubic lice. They disappear when the lice are treated.

3. Salmon patches
These pink marks appear commonly on the nape of the neck, the eyelids, above the nose, and the midforehead of newborns. They are sometimes referred to as an "angel's kiss" or a "stork bite."

4. Strawberry marks (hemangiomas)
These lesions are usually not present at birth but appear during the first four to six weeks of life.

D. Folk Practices
Vietnamese children sometimes present with linear bruises of the chest and back which, although they resemble abuse, are actually the result of the folk-medicine practice *Cao Gio*. In this practice, used to relieve symptoms such as fever, chills, and headaches, the skin is massaged with oil and stroked with the edge of a coin until bruising occurs. Normally, this practice should not cause undue concern about child abuse. Adherence to this practice when a child is seriously ill, with refusal to seek medical care, may raise a question of medical neglect.

REFERENCES

Adler, R., & Kane-Nussen, B. (1983). Erythema multiforme: Confusion with child battering syndrome. *Pediatrics, 72,* 718.

Bays, J. (1994). Conditions mistaken for child abuse. In R. Reece (Ed.), *Child abuse: Medical diagnosis and management.* Philadelphia, PA: Lea & Febiger.

Ellerstein, N. (1981). Dermatologic manifestations of child abuse and neglect. In N. Ellerstein (Ed.), *Child abuse and neglect: A medical reference.* New York: John Wiley & Sons.

Ellerstein, N. (1979). The cutaneous manifestations of child abuse and neglect. *American Journal of Diseases of Children, 133,* 906.

Jacobs, A., & Walton, R.G. (1976). The incidence of birthmarks in the neonate. *Pediatrics, 58,* 218.

Maurice, P., & Cream, J. (1989). The dangers of herbalism. *British Medical Journal, 299,* 1204.

O'Hare, A.E., & Eden, O.B. (1984). Bleeding disorders and nonaccidental injury. *Archives of Disease in Childhood, 59,* 860.

Schmitt, B. (1987). The child with nonaccidental trauma. In R. Helfer & R. Kempe (Eds.), *The battered child.* Chicago, IL: The University of Chicago Press.

Spitz, W.U., & Fisher, R.S., (Eds.). (1926). *Medicolegal investigation of death: Guidelines for the application of pathology to criminal investigation.* Springfield, IL: Charles C. Thomas Publisher.

Sterne, G.G., et al. (1986). Oral and dental aspects of child abuse and neglect. *Pediatrics, 78,* 537.

Wilson, E.F. (1977). Estimation of the age of cutaneous contusions in child abuse. *Pediatrics, 60,* 750.

Yeatman, G., et al. (1976). Pseudobattering in Vietnamese children. *Pediatrics, 58,* 616.

ABUSE BY BURNS

Although burns are a common cause of unintentional injury, they also account for 6 to 16% of child abuse cases. The National Safety Council reports that burns are the fourth most frequent cause of death in children under the age of five, and the third most frequent cause of death in children up to the age of 14. The number of childhood burns determined as abusive varies from 6 to 28%. Boys are more commonly victims of both burn accidents and abuse; the peak age is usually around two to three years. Although abusive burns can occur in any shape or form, there are some particular patterns which occur more frequently, such as immersion burns, splash burns, and contact burns. Others include chemical, electrical, and microwave burns. It is important to know what to look for in the physician's diagnosis and treatment of the burn, as well as some common indicators of abuse.

I. Medical Terminology Used in Burn Injuries

In assessing a burn, the doctor will usually make note of its severity, the extent of the body covered, and its exact location. Each of these determinations is documented in a customary way. It is useful for you to understand the significance of these findings.

A. Severity

The severity of burn injuries is categorized into four degrees, depending on the number of layers of skin injured.

1. *First degree burns*

A superficial burn of minimal depth. Characterized by *erythema* (redness), *hyperemia* (redness which disappears under pressure), tenderness, and swelling. Although not usually severe, these burns can be serious if they cover a large percentage of body area. An example would be a sunburn.

2. *Second degree burns*

A burn extending through the *epidermis* (the outermost layer) and into the *dermis* (the next layer). Characterized by *vesicles* (weeping blisters) on the skin's surface with increased sensitivity to touch. If no infection occurs, these injuries usually take from 14 to 21 days to heal. When severe, they can sometimes require surgery.

3. *Third degree burns*

The entire thickness of the skin is burned, (epidermis and dermis), including the hair follicles. The area looks white or charred and is not sensitive to touch or pin prick. These injuries require hospitalization and often require skin grafting. These burns heal with scarring, creating a change in color and a "parchment" type of skin.

4. *Fourth degree burns*

The depth of these burns extend into the muscles, bones, and joints.

B. Extent

The extent of the burn is another important factor in determining its severity. For example, a superficial burn which covers a large part of the body is more serious than a third degree burn which covers a small part of the body. Physicians express the extent of burns in percentages of total body surface area covered. First degree burns are not included in this measurement. Remember that a burn which may cover only a small area of an adult could cover an appreciably larger area of an infant's body. Notice the difference in percentage of surface area on children and adults.

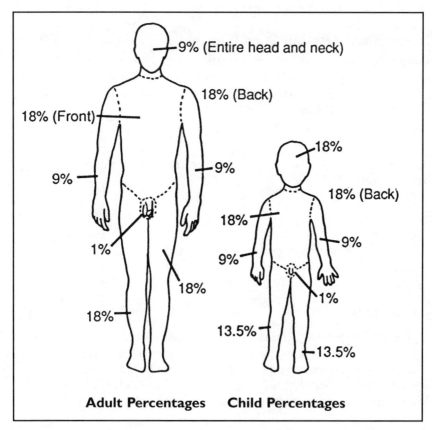

9% (Entire head and neck)
18% (Back)
18% (Front)
9%
9%
1%
18%
18%
18%
18% (Back)
18%
9%
9%
1%
13.5%
13.5%

Adult Percentages   Child Percentages

Burns are considered severe when they cover:

- over 10% of the body in children under two years old.
- over 15% of the body in children between two and twelve years old.
- over 20% of the body in children of any age.
- any burn of the face, hands, or genitalia.

Burns covering over 65% of the body are sometimes fatal, even when only first degree. The exact location of the burn will usually be documented in the physician's report by an actual diagram. These locations are important factors in determining the likelihood of abuse. Accidental burns are most likely to occur on the front of the head, neck, trunk, and arms. Those found on the back of the head, neck, chest, extremities, and genitalia are rarely self-inflicted and are very likely abusive.

II. The Importance of the History

A detailed history is especially important in determining the etiology of a burn. When acquiring the history and subsequently relating it to the doctor, remember to include the following:

- Who was involved in the incident? What is his or her developmental maturity? (i.e., Was the child mature enough to have done what was alleged?)

- When exactly did the act occur? If there was a delay in seeking treatment, why? (Physicians can usually estimate the age of burns to tell if they have really "recently occurred.")

In cases of suspected *immersion burns*, remember to ask:

- What was the container in which the child was immersed? (Tubs produce areas of nonburn whereas pots on hot burners do not.)

- How deep was the liquid in the container?

- What was the exact position of the child's body when the incident occurred?

- What was the estimated temperature of the liquid?

In the case of *splash burns*, remember to ask the following:

- How far did the liquid travel in the air before hitting the child? (Across the room? From the stove to the floor?)

- What was the exact position of the child's body when the incident occurred?

- What was the child wearing when the incident occurred? Were the clothes removed immediately?

- What exactly was the liquid which splashed the victim? Was it greasy?

Although children who die from clothing ignition or from being trapped in burning rooms, trailers, etc. are excluded from investigation by CPS workers, you may want to investigate the living conditions of siblings remaining i the home, especially if abuse has been previously suspected there. There have been cases in which parents or caretakers attempt to burn their children to death in order to "destroy the evidence" of previously inflicted injuries, either psychological or physical. Any burns which occur with one or more of the following should have a complete examination for abuse.

- A history incompatible with the physical findings.

- A burn incompatible with the developmental age of the child.

- Burns assessed as older than the historical account.

- Nutritional neglect.

- Unrelated hematomas, lacerations, and scars.

- Old long bone or skull fractures found on skeletal survey.

- Burns attributed to siblings (although these do occur accidentally).

- An adult not present at the incident seeking medical attention.

- Treatment delay of 24 hours or more.

- A previous history of burns.

III. Immersion Burns

A. Temperature of Tap Water and Related Burn Times

Scalding burns account for 25 to 28% of all abusive burns in children. Below 120° F, hot water is unlikely to inflict major injury. At a temperature of 127° F, it can cause full thickness burns, through the epidermis, in one minute. At 130° F, burns will occur within 30 seconds, and at 150° F, within two seconds. Remember also that these figures are for adults; above 140° F, a child's skin can burn four times as fast as that of an adult. How do these numbers relate to the average household? In a year's survey of average tap-water temperatures in Seattle homes, it was determined that 80% had bathtub water temperatures greater than 130° F, with an average temperature of 142° F. With the availability of water at such high temperatures, it is not surprising that scalds are common forms of both accidental and abusive burns. While it was once common to preset new electric heaters at 150° F and gas heaters at 140° F, this is no longer true.

Many states have recently enacted legislation lowering preset temperatures on new heaters to 120-125° F. In homes in which the high temperature of the water seems to be a problem, physicians can suggest that a family lower its preset temperature to the minimum. Many apartment dwellers have little choice about water temperature settings. You can help prevent nonintentional tap water burns by assisting the family in their efforts to request adjustment of the hot water heater by the local gas or electric company.

B. Patterns

Immersion burns usually occur when parts of the body are forced into hot water, usually from a running tap or in a filled tub. Usually the restrained child cannot move in the liquid, thus the burns leave clear lines of demarcation on the skin.

1. *Hands and Feet*

Hands and feet which have been forcefully held under water usually have symmetrical, "stocking" or "glove" patterns which are uniform in depth. Often the child will tripod onto her hands and feet to try to protect the rest of her body. The palms of the hands and sole of the feet have particularly thick skin, usually resistant to thermal damage. Any full thickness burns to these areas should be suspected as abusive. (See Figures 1 and 2)

Figure I

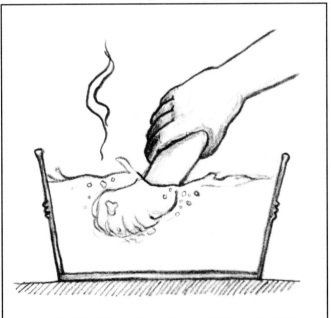

Figure 2

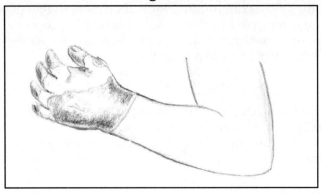

2. *Perineum*

Another common scald pattern is seen on the perineum, the area between the vagina and anus in the female and the scrotum and anus in the male. These burns are often inflicted as a form of punishment for the child who is not yet toilet trained. In an effort to both clean and punish the child, the caretaker will often hold him in a "jack-knifed" position, in which his knees are held against his chest, forcing his perineum under hot running water or dunking it into a tub or pot of hot water. There are several ways to tell if this type of burn has occurred.

a. *"Doughnut Hole"*

A child who has been forced into a porcelain or fiberglass tub will often have parts of his body, usually the buttocks, resting on the bottom of the tub. Because this area is in contact with the cool tub instead of the hot water, it will not burn, thus creating a patch of unburned skin in the center of the burn, much like a "doughnut-hole." (See Figure 3)

Figure 3

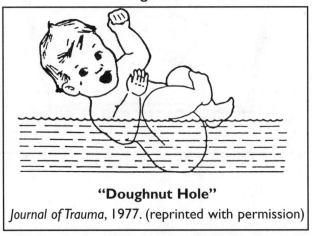

"Doughnut Hole"
Journal of Trauma, 1977. (reprinted with permission)

b. *Parallel Lines*

In this type of pattern, there is a uniform burn in all areas exposed to the liquid. A distinct line separates the skin area that has been exposed from that which has not. These lines can be made parallel by positioning the body into the estimated position of the child at the time of immersion. A careful examination of these patterns can often lead to the diagnosis of abuse.

c. *Flexion*

Often the burned area will have a "zebra-stripe" appearance, in which there are stripes of unburned skin in the middle of the burned area. These "stripes" occur at the areas of flexion which were bent while the body came into contact with the liquid. Because the skin in these areas is pressed against other areas of skin, it does not come into contact with the liquid and is thus spared of burning.

Differential - Accidental Immersions

It would not be unusual for a child who has fallen into a hot tub to raise herself onto her hands and feet in an effort to regain balance and to climb out of the heat. Such an accident could create burns similar to those in forced immersion. However, there are some differences in these types of patterns.

- Accidental burns have no clear line demarcating the burned and unburned skin, nor will the burns be symmetrical on both hands or both feet. Children will thrash around, creating uneven patterns on each limb.

- Accidental burns will not be as deep as forced burns, for an unrestrained child will rarely be unable to remove himself from the burning environment.

- Any burns which involve just the perineum and possibly the feet, with no burning of the hands, should be questioned, for it is almost impossible for a child to fall into a tub in this position accidentally.

- A parent or caretaker who claims that he or she tested the water and "thought it was all right" should arouse suspicion. Adults find water to be uncomfortable at temperatures around 109° F, while temperatures must be above 120° F to cause full thickness burns in a short amount of time.

- Although accidental burns are not an uncommon occurrence in any household, too many or improperly handled accidents can be indicators of neglect. Parents/caretakers who refuse to watch their children in the kitchen or refuse to put protective screens around wood stoves or heaters may only need to be educated. Others might be too irresponsible or uncaring to warrant leaving the child in the home. Children in these neglectful environments live at a high risk of being seriously injured, and should be carefully considered for placement in alternate care.

IV. Splash Burns

In splash burns, a hot liquid is either thrown or poured onto the victim. The depth of the burn in these cases is usually not as deep as that seen in immersion burns, because the liquid usually cools as it falls through the air (a good reason to know the distance). Usually there are several small, scattered, "satellite" burns in this situation. Splash burns are usually not as severe or as thick as immersion burns, because the liquid runs off the skin before it has a chance to deeply damage it. The area which comes into contact with the main mass of fluid is usually the area of deepest burn. Often the pattern is an "arrowhead" configuration. It is usually possible to estimate the direction from which the liquid came, as well as the position of the body.

Differential - Accidental Splash Burns

When determining the etiology of splash burns, look closely at the area of the body covered by the burn. Self-induced accidental burns rarely can occur from behind. Accidental burns, such as those occurring from a hot liquid being pulled from the stove, are most likely to occur on the front of the head, neck, trunk, and arms. Rarely are those found on the back of the head, neck, chest, and extremities in self-inflicted accidents. Another factor to look for is the extent of the burn and its compatibility with the history of the accident. If a parent or caretaker has spilled a cup of coffee on a child, the burns should not cover a large percentage of the body area. An average coffee cup simply does not hold enough liquid to cause a large extent of damage. If the child suffers from extensive burns on a large percentage of total surface body area, the history should be compatible in terms of the amount of liquid involved.

V. Contact Burns

Contact burns are the second most frequent cause of abusive burns. These burns are always at least second degree burns. It is often easy to identify the object of contact from the shape of the burn.

A. Cigarette Burns

Cigarette burns are one type of contact burn frequently seen in abuse. These burns measure about 1 cm in diameter and are often found in multiples on the trunk, external genitalia, and extremities, such as the palms of the hands and the soles of the feet. Depending on the duration of contact, these can be anything from blisters to excavated wounds. Healed cigarette burns may appear as either hyper- (darkened) or hypo- (absent) pigmented areas of the skin. Sometimes, however, they may leave no residual traces.

> ### Differential - Accidental Cigarette Burns
>
> It is not uncommon for a child to brush against a cigarette which is being held in someone else's hand. These burns are usually found on the child's face, arms, or trunk, depending on the height of the child and the height of the person holding the cigarette. An accidental burn is usually more elongated than round, with a higher degree of intensity on one side, due to the effect of brushing past the lighted tip. Usually the history should verify this possibility.
>
> Often the blisters produced by the skin disease impetigo are similar in appearance to cigarette burns. Impetigo blisters usually do not leave scars, whereas cigarette burns may. Remember also that impetigo can occur as a result of cigarette burns if the wounds go untreated. Suspicious blisters will generally be cultured by the practitioner for streptococcal infections that may be found with impetigo and treated with antibiotics.

B. Burns by objects

Some common instruments seen in abusive situations are irons, stove burners, heater grates, radiators, electric hot plates, curling irons, and hair dryers. A study of electric hair dryers showed that at high heat, dryers held stationary approximately three inches from the skin are capable of producing a full thickness burn in 1 to 10 seconds, dependent upon the power level of the dryer. In most instances, dryers are kept in constant motion to avoid overheating the skin. In addition, the protective grid on many dryers is capable of producing a second degree burn within 1 to 2 seconds for as long as 2 minutes after the dryers are turned off. In some burns, objects such as combs, keys, knives, or cigarette lighters are heated and "branded" into the skin. Like cigarette burns, there are some typical patterns which can help in determining the etiology of these types of burns.

VI. Chemical / Electrical / Microwave Burns

A. Chemical

Chemical burns are often deeper and more severe than scalding burns. This is because the burning process continues as long as the substance is in contact with the skin, as opposed to scalding burns, in which the water cools, evaporates, or eventually runs off of the body. Clothing impregnated by kerosene, acetic acid, and other mild irritants has been shown to produce lesions resembling first and second degree burns when the material remains in contact with the skin for a period of time.

B. Electrical

The U.S. Child Protective Services Committee estimates that each year there occur more than 4,000 child electrical injuries requiring emergency care. The majority of children with these burns are under five years of age. Most occur from the conduction of current through the saliva of a child who is sucking or mouthing the plug. A child who bites a live electric cord will usually have characteristic burns at the corners of the mouth. These burns often present as deep injuries.

C. Microwave

Burns resulting from microwave ovens are very deep, affecting both the skin and the deep muscle layers, which have a greater water content and burn more quickly. Layers of fat are relatively spared during the burning. Often the tissue is actually charred in this situation.

VII. Folk Practices

There are several folk-medicine treatments which tend to cause burns that may appear abusive. It is helpful to be aware of the most common of these practices and the types of burns which they inflict. Physicians and social workers must use their own discretion in treating these families. Ultimately you will have to weigh the importance of the family unity with the safety of the child in the home. Frequently these families need only to be educated about the hazards of their practices.

In one case a child presented with second and third degree scalds on the foot and ankle. It was found that her Puerto Rican foster mother had applied a large amount of the analgesic balm "Icy Hot" to her foot and held it under running water. This home treatment, based on a hot-cold theory of disease held in many Latin American cultures, was performed in an effort to cure the child's sprained ankle. Because there was a clear line of demarcation between the burned and unburned skin, it looked as though her foot had been held under hot water.

Some Mexican-Americans believe in a practice called "cupping," in which a cup of ignited alcohol is placed over an affected part of the body. As the heated area cools, the skin is sucked up into the cup, producing redness and burns. These burns are circular, about 6-8 cm in diameter, and are often multiple.

Southeast Asian children will sometimes present with burns or scars which look like cigarette burns. These are usually .5 -1 cm in diameter, and are located randomly around the lower rib cage or in a definite pattern around the umbilicus, or "belly button." These burns are part of a folk medical therapy in which pieces of burning string are lowered onto the child's skin, supposedly to cure abdominal pain or fever.

At least one case of second degree burns, coupled with inhalation pneumonia, has been reported as a result of fabric dipped in kerosene and applied to the skin in an attempt to treat upper respiratory congestion.

As stated previously, these folk-medicine remedies might be considered abusive if they occur repeatedly under severe conditions. If the parents or caretakers do not respond to counseling and education regarding these injuries, you should consider removing the child from the home.

VIII. Treatment and Placement Decisions

The child should receive immediate medical evaluation if:

- The burn is over 10% of the body of an infant less than two years old.

- The burn is over 15% of the body of children between two to twelve years old.

- The burn is over 20% of the body of children of any age.

- There are facial or perineal/genital burns.

• There are third degree burns.

One of the first decisions a practitioner will make in the medical evaluation is whether or not to hospitalize the child. This usually occurs when a victim has second or third degree burns. Remember that victims who are not hospitalized, and those who are returning home after hospitalization, will still need special care. In your assessment of a child's posttreatment placement, you should consider the ability of the parent or caretaker to perform the following treatments:

• *Dressing Changes*
Can the parent/caretaker understand and perform the mechanics of the dressing changes? Is he/she psychologically fit to view and care for the wounds? Is the environment sanitary enough to avoid infection?

• *Emotional Support*
Because burn injuries are exceptionally painful and debilitating, the victim needs a lot of support and reassurance at this time; the caretaker must be aware and sensitive to his special needs.

• *Subsequent Treatment*
Treatment of the burned child continues long after acute care has healed the wounds. As he grows and develops, the child will need continuous evaluations and often surgeries to reconstruct the contractures of healing skin. Hospital burn units usually have their own social workers who will be able to work with you in the follow-up care of the child.

REFERENCES

Alexander, R.C., Surrell, J.A., & Cohle, S.D. (1987). Microwave oven burns in children: An unusual manifestation of child abuse. *Pediatrics, 79,* 255.

Bays, J. (1994), Conditions mistaken for child abuse. In R. Reece (Ed.), *Child abuse: Medical diagnosis and management.* Philadelphia, PA: Lea & Febiger.

Crikelair, G.G., & Dhaliwal, A.S. (1976). The cause and prevention of electrical burns of the mouth in children. *Plastic Reconstructive Surgery, 58,* 206.

Crikelair, F.F., Symonds, F.C., Ollstein, R.N., & Kirsner, A.I. (1968). Burn causation: Its many sides. *Journal of Trauma, 8,* 572.

Deitch, E.A. & Staats, M. (1982). Child abuse through burning. *Journal of Burn Care and Rehabilitation, 3,* 89.

Ellerstein, N. (1979). The cutaneous manifestations of child abuse and neglect. *American Journal of Diseases of Children, 133,* 906.

Feldman, K. (1984). Pseudoabusive burns in Asian refugees. *American Journal of Diseases of Children, 138,* 768.

Feldman, K., Schaller, R., Feldman, J., & McMillon, M. (1978). Tap water scald burns in children. *Pediatrics, 62,* 1.

Hight, D., Bakatar, H., & Lloyd, J. (1979). Inflicted burns in children: Recognition and treatment. *Journal of the American Medical Association, 242,* 517.

Hobbs, C.J. (1986). When are burns not accidental? *Archives of Diseases of Children, 61,* 357.

Lenoski, E.F., & Hunter, K.A. (1977). Specific patterns of inflicted burns in children. *The Journal of Trauma, 17,* 842.

McLoughlin, E., & Crawford, J.D. (1985). Burns. *Pediatrics Clinics of North American, 32,* 61.

Moritz, A., & Henriques, F. (1947). Studies of thermal injury: The relative importance of time and surface temperature in the causation of cutaneous burns. *American Journal of Pathology, 23,* 695.

Mosconi, G., et al. (1988). Kerosene "burns": A new case. *Contact Dermatitis, 19,* 314.

Nussinovitch, M., et al. (1992). Chemical pneumonia and dermatitis caused by kerosene. (Letter) *Clinical Pediatrics, 31,* 574.

Prescott, P.R. (1990). Hair dryer burns in children. *Pediatrics, 86,* 692.

Sandler, A.P., & Hayes, V. (1978). Nonaccidental trauma and medical folk belief: A case of cupping. *Pediatrics,61,* 921.

Schanberger, J. (1981). Inflicted burns in children. *Topics in Emergency Medicine,* 85.

Schmitt, B., Gray, J., & Britton, H. (1978). Car seat burns in infants: Avoiding confusion with inflicted burns. *Pediatrics, 62,* 607.

Watkins, A., Gagan, R., & Cupoli, M. (1985). Child abuse by burning. *Florida Medical Association, 72,* 497.

ABUSIVE FRACTURES

It is now estimated that abuse accounts for 20% of the skeletal trauma seen in children. As early as 1946, Dr. John Caffey made the connection between unexplained fractures and the Battered Child Syndrome. With the use of radiology, we can not only confirm that a fracture exists, but also gain insight into how it was produced. One distinctive feature of abusive fractures is that they most commonly occur in children below the age of two.

In the determination of abuse, you must work closely with the physician, combining details of the history with the evidence of radiology to distinguish accidental fractures from abusive ones. The following hints can make this process a relatively easy one.

I. When to Suspect Abuse

When investigating a case for child abuse, it is important to pay detailed attention to the history, such as the exact date of the injury and the way in which the incident occurred. Often, the physician will be able to confirm or disprove the legitimacy of the history through radiology (the use of X-rays). You should be suspicious of abuse when any of the following occur:

- Unsuspected fractures are "accidentally" discovered in the course of an examination.

- The skeletal injury is out of proportion with the history given.

- Multiple fractures, which are often symmetrical, exist.

- Multiple fractures in various stages of healing exist.

- Skeletal trauma is accompanied by injuries, for example, burns, to other parts of the body.

- Note: absence of bruising at the fracture site is irrelevant in deciding whether or not a fracture is nonaccidental.

With the aid of radiology and a physician skilled at interpreting X-rays, the examiner can form a fairly precise picture of where a fracture exists, what kind of fracture exists, and its age.

II. Medical Terminology

A. Bones of infants and children

A physician's first step in investigating a fracture is determining its location and its type. This determination can often help uncover the etiology of the fracture. It is a good idea to refer to a skeletal diagram if you are uncertain of the location of a particular bone. Remember that some bones have two names. For example, a "collar bone" is also called a *clavicle*, and a "shoulder blade" is also called a *scapula*. *Long bones* refer to bones of the legs and arms.

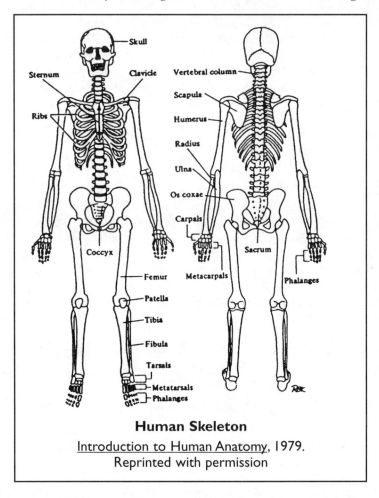

Human Skeleton
Introduction to Human Anatomy, 1979.
Reprinted with permission

Long bones are divided into three distinct sections. The *diaphysis* refers to the shaft, or midportion of the bone. The *epiphysis* refers to the end of the bone. In a growing child, these ends are separated from the diaphysis by a layer of cartilage, called the *epiphyseal plate*, or *metaphysis*. As the bone grows, this cartilage slowly produces more and more compact bone, causing the bone to lengthen. This growth plate is one of the weakest areas of the child's bone and is a common area of injury in child abuse. The outer covering of the bone, the *periosteum*, contains blood vessels and special cells that help in repair following an injury. The *distal* portion of the bone refers to the end farthest from the person's trunk, while the *proximal* end refers to that closest to the trunk. *Posterior* means towards the rear. *Lateral* pertains to the side, while *bilateral* pertains to both sides.

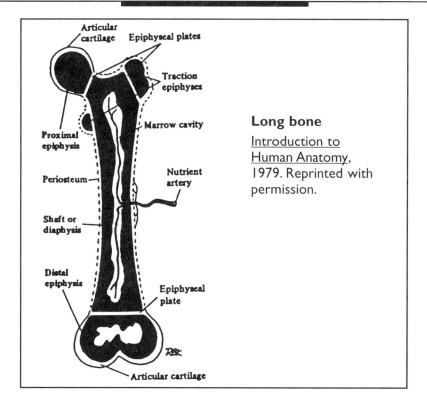

Articular cartilage
Epiphyseal plates
Traction epiphyses
Marrow cavity
Proximal epiphysis
Periosteum
Nutrient artery
Shaft or diaphysis
Distal epiphysis
Epiphyseal plate
Articular cartilage

Long bone
Introduction to Human Anatomy, 1979. Reprinted with permission.

B. Types of fractures

The list of names for particular types of fractures is very detailed; however, you should be familiar with some of the major terms which physicians use in describing a break.

- *Closed fracture* – a fracture of the bone with no skin wound.

- *Complicated fracture* – a fracture in which the broken bone has injured some internal organ.

- *Compound fracture* – a fracture in which the bone is broken and protruding from the skin.

- *Compression fracture* – a collapse of the bone along the direction of force.

- *Displaced fracture* – a fracture in which the broken ends are not in alignment

- *Greenstick fracture* – a fracture in which the bone is partially bent and partially broken, as when a green stick breaks. It occurs in children, especially those with rickets.

- *Hairline fracture* – a minor fracture in which all the portions of the bone are in perfect alignment.

- *Impacted fracture* – a fracture in which the bone is broken, and (buckle fracture) one end is wedged into the interior of the other end.

- *Metaphyseal fracture* – a chip of the growing end of a bone pulled off by a ligament. This fracture usually comes from shaking. (See Figure 1)

- *Pathologic fracture* – a fracture of a diseased or weakened bone, produced by a force that would not have fractured a healthy bone.

- *Spiral fracture* — a slanting, diagonal fracture. (See Figure 1)

- *Transverse fracture* – a fracture in which the fracture line is at right angles to the long axis of the bone. (See Figure 1)

Figure I

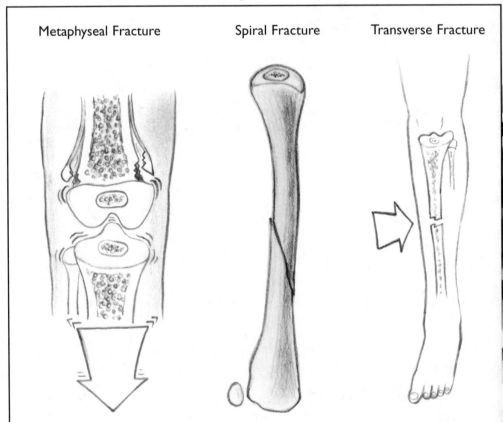

Metaphyseal Fracture   Spiral Fracture   Transverse Fracture

III. Specific Mechanisms of Abuse and Their Consequences

The following table is adapted from Leonard Swischuk's (1981) breakdown of common mechanisms resulting in abusive injuries.

Mechanism	Area injured	Type of fracture
direct blow	extremities	transverse, diaphyseal injuries
	clavicle	midshaft fracture
	face	facial, jaw fractures
	abdomen	injuries to internal organs
	chest	rib fractures, internal injuries
twisting force	long bones	spiral fracture
		metaphyseal fractures
shaking	skull	discussed later in"head injuries"
	long bones	metaphyseal fractures
	spine	various injuries
squeezing	chest	bilateral fractures of ribs

IV. Dating the Fracture

Dating a fracture is one of the most important steps in determining its origin. Whenever the date of the history does not coincide with the age of the fracture, you should be suspicious of abuse. In determining the date of a fracture, the physician will examine any soft tissue damage, such as bruises or lacerations, the visibility of the fracture line on an X-ray, the stage of the *callus* (the new bone forming around the fracture), and the changes in the *periosteal new bone* (the outer covering of the bone which helps in repair). In very young children, signs of old fractures can sometimes disappear entirely after six months to a year. Remember that at first, subtle or hairline fractures may be difficult to discern on an X-ray, because the bone has not yet had time to form a callus. Some general guidelines in determining the age are:

- 0 to 10 days — No signs of fracture present, only swelling.

- 10 days to 8 weeks — Callus formation, epiphyseal thickening, periosteal thickening in the injured area.

- 8 weeks — Periosteum begins to blend back into old bone.

V. Different X-rays and the Appropriateness of their Use

Skeletal radiography (X-ray) is the main "tool" which a physician uses to determine the location, age, and cause of a suspected fracture. Although these procedures are usually benign, they should not be done unless indicated. The physician will avoid exposing the child to unnecessary amounts of radiation by keeping records of his X-rays. If it is necessary to take a child to another physician, be sure to request that all of his medical records, including his X-rays or copies of the X-rays, be sent to that physician. Do not assume that this will be done without your request.

A. Skeletal survey

This is an X-ray procedure in which the entire skeleton, including the skull, thoracic cage, spine, and extremities, is radiographed to determine the presence of fractures in any part of the body.

The skeletal survey should be a routine part of the medical evaluation of children less than two years old when there is suspicion of physical abuse, and in infants less than one year old when there are signs of significant neglect. Between the ages of two and five, the survey should be done selectively, based upon the clinical presentation and history. Beyond the age of five, acute hidden fractures are rare, so the survey is of little diagnostic value. The general rule to keep in mind is that the less the child is able to tell about where he or she hurts, the greater the value of the skeletal survey.

B. Bone scan

Also referred to as a *radionuclide skeletal scintography*, this is a process in which radioactive substances are injected into the bloodstream. The scintillations, or "heat" from these radionuclides is then photographed in those areas of new bone growth. The advantage of this method is that it can detect fractures within 24 hours after they occur, whereas conventional X-rays may take as long as 8 to 10 days for detection. This process is especially helpful in determining rib fractures and periosteal (bone lining) injuries. It is not a good method, however, for reviewing metaphyseal fractures, because these occur at a site where there is a lot of growing bone, injured or not. This method also lacks sensitivity in detecting skull and vertebral fractures. Bone scans are typically quite expensive in small hospitals, where they are used infrequently.

There are possible situations in which a skeletal survey is not recommended, such as cases of suspected sexual abuse in which no signs of physical abuse are recognized, or soft tissue injuries to older children who are quite capable of reporting physical injuries.

VI. Areas of the Body Commonly Associated with Abuse

A. Extremities

Fractures of the extremities account for 77% of all those seen in abused children. These are most likely to occur in the long bones of the arms and legs, and are not as common in the hands and feet. These fractures commonly present as transverse or spiral fractures of the diaphysis and as metaphyseal fractures. Spiral fractures in a child who cannot yet walk should raise suspicion. Metaphyseal fractures should always be investigated for abuse, for they cannot occur from falling down, but only from having a jerking force applied to the extremities; these are seen in shaking injuries. Remember, however, that a caretaker who grabs a child to save him from a dangerous fall could cause the same amount of damage as one who is abusing his child. In these cases, only the history can offer clues to the real etiology of the injury.

Differential – Accident vs. Abuse

• Birthing Trauma — Clavicular and humeral (both shaft and epiphyseal) fractures are frequently found in newborn babies, especially those from breech deliveries. If an infant over 11 days old shows fractures with no signs of healing, they should be considered as occurring after birth. (Swischuk, 1981)

• Little League Elbow — Frequently, epiphyseal separations occur when a child continually flexes his elbow in the action of throwing a ball. The age of the child and the history can usually exclude this possibility.

• Infants receiving passive exercises for therapeutic reasons have been known to sustain fractures of the extremities when a caretaker administers them improperly. This problem should present itself in the history, and deserves immediate attention.

B. Ribs / Sternum

Rib fractures are another common injury seen in abusive incidents, with almost 90% seen in children under two years of age. Usually, the ribcage is compliant under mild pressure. Therefore, any fractures of this area should be considered the product of major unintentional trauma or abuse.

Most inflicted rib fractures are now thought to be the result of shaking rather than direct blows or lateral compression of the chest. The assailant's palms are usually laterally placed, with thumbs in front and fingers at the back. Compression is from front to back, with initial fractures occurring next to the spine and additional fractures occurring laterally as the pressure increases. Because the compression forces are more or less uniform during shaking, the fractures are often multiple and bilateral. Direct blows in older children may result in rib fractures at the point of impact.

Fractures of the sternum (breast bone) are rarely reported in abused infants and children, but when present, they are pathognomonic (indicative) of abuse.

Differential – Accident vs. Abuse

• Children sustaining severe trauma requiring CPR may present with rib fractures attributed to the administration of CPR. It has been found, however, that although these injuries do occur in adults, children do not receive rib fractures from CPR, and should be considered as receiving them from some other source.

C. Skull fractures

These fractures are a common manifestation of child abuse, and can be very serious. The next chapter, "Injuries to the Head, Eyes, Ears, Nose, and Mouth," covers this topic in detail.

D. Vertebral fractures

Although they are not as common as fractures of the extremities or skull, vertebral fractures are another type of injury seen in abuse. These can occur from forced bending of the spine, or hyperflexion, a process which can cause the discs between the vertebrae to painfully pinch into the spinal cord. These abuses are seen most often in children under two years old, and are usually associated with other injuries to the limbs. The physician may refer to "hooked" or "notched" vertebrae as indicators of this type of injury. In some cases, vertebral injuries may be caused by Whiplash Shaken Infant Syndrome. Symptoms of neurologic injury may be vomiting, a loss of weight, irritability, and slowed development. Often, however, no neurologic signs of injury exist, and the spinal lesions go unrecognized.

VII. Differentials

In addition to considering accidental trauma as a cause of fractures, the physician may test for various organic abnormalities, such as genetic problems or bone diseases, as possible causes for the radiological findings.

A. Congenital Syphilis

This disease causes bone irregularities similar to trauma, not only as a result of the disease itself, but also as a result of a weakening of the bone, which makes it more susceptible to damage.

B. Infantile Cortical Hyperostosis (Caffey's Disease)

This skeletal abnormality typically presents itself in infants up to two to three months old with red, painful, swollen extremities. One diagnostic feature is that 95% of the bone abnormalities caused by this disease involve the mandible or jaw.

C. Leukemia

A severe disease of the blood-forming organs, including the bone marrow associated with progressive anemia, internal hemorrhage, and exhaustion.

D. Menke's Kinky Hair Syndrome

This syndrome, resulting from a deficiency in copper metabolism, results in symmetrical problems in the shaft (diaphysis) and the ends (metaphysis) of the bone. Often associated with failure to thrive, Menke's Kinky Hair Syndrome is also associated with seizures, psychomotor retardation, and progressive neurologic degeneration. Its name is derived from the characteristic sparse, kinky hair which appears at a few months.

E. Osteogenesis Imperfecta (OI)

Of all the various conditions suggested by caretakers and their legal representatives to explain inflicted fractures, this is the most frequently cited. It is an inherited disorder of connective tissue leading to abnormal bone formation and increased fragility. Various types of OI have other clinical features, such as short stature, blue sclera, wormian bones in the skull, hearing loss, etc. While severe cases may manifest themselves in the newborn period with extensive fractures, others may not be apparent for months or even years. Connective tissue biopsy may be instrumental in confirming the diagnosis of OI in atypical cases. This, however, is rarely necessary.

When entertaining the possibility of OI in a case of suspected child abuse, the pediatrician, orthopedist, geneticist, and radiologist must work together in a coordinated effort to arrive at the proper diagnosis. In the presence of unexplained fractures or fractures typical for child abuse, the possibility of OI is unlikely without the presence of some other associated clinical feature of OI. The key to distinction is the correlation of clinical history, physical examination, family history, and radiologic findings.

F. Osteomyelitis

Bacterial bone infections can produce skeletal changes that resemble fractures.

G. Rickets

Although fractures are not a common result of infantile nutritional rickets, this deficiency can cause other irregularities in the bones similar to those caused by trauma.

H. Scurvy

Resulting from vitamin C deficiency, scurvy can cause irregularities and fractures of the bones. It is generalized, meaning it affects all of the bones of the body, and is usually accompanied by bruising and swelling of the extremities. Scurvy is extremely rare before the age of six months.

It is important to remember that these diseases are all quite infrequent. Despite these other diagnoses, nonaccidental trauma (child abuse) accounts for 11% to 55% of the skeletal trauma seen in children. Keep in mind the significance of the age of the child in these statistics. Over 80% of abusive fractures occur in children below the age of eighteen months, while only 2% of the accidental fractures occur in this age group.

REFERENCES

Ablin, D., et al. (1990). Differentiation of child abuse from osteogenisis imperfecta. *American Journal of Roentgenology, 154,* 1035.

American Academy of Pediatric Section on Radiology Recommendations. (1991, February). Diagnostic imaging of child abuse. *Pediatrics, 87,* 262.

Baron, M.A., Bejar, R., & Shaeff, P. (1970). Neurologic manifestations of the battered child syndrome. *Pediatrics, 45,* 1005.

Caffey, J. (1946). Multiple fractures in the long bones of infants suffering from chronic subdural hematoma. *American Journal of Roentgenology, 56,* 163.

Cullen, J.C. (1975). Spinal lesions in battered babies. *The Journal of Bone and Joint Surgery, 33,* 364.

Feldman, J., & Brewer, D. (1984). Child abuse, cardiopulmonary resuscitation, and rib fractures. *Pediatrics, 72,* 339.

Helfer, R., et al. (1984). Trauma to the bones of small infants from passive exercise: A factor in the etiology of child abuse. *The Journal of Pediatrics, 104,* 47.

Leonidas, J.C. (1983). Skeletal trauma in the child abuse syndrome. *Pediatric Annals, 12,* 875.

Merten, D., et al. (1994). Skeletal manifestations of child abuse. In R. Reece (Ed.), *Child abuse: Medical diagnosis and management.* Philadelphia, PA: Lea & Febiger.

Merten, D., Radkowski, M., & Leonidas, J. (1983). The abused child: A radiological reappraisal. *Radiology, 146,* 377.

Radkowski, M. (1983). The battered child syndrome: Pitfalls in radiological diagnosis. *Pediatric Annals, 12,* 294.

Swischuk, L. (1981). Radiology of the skeletal system. In N. Ellerstein (Ed.), *Child abuse and neglect: A medical reference.* New York: John Wiley & Sons.

Swischuk, L. (1969). Spine and spinal cord trauma in the battered child syndrome. *Radiology, 92,* 733.

Worlock, P., Stower, M., & Barbor, P. (1986). Patterns of fractures in accidental and nonaccidental injury in children: A comparative study. *British Medical Journal, 293,* 100.

INJURIES TO THE HEAD, EYES, EARS, NOSE, AND MOUTH

Trauma to the skull and brain is the primary cause of mortality in child abuse today. Over 95% of serious intracranial injuries during the first year of life are the result of physical abuse. Children under two years of age are characteristically at the greatest risk for this type of trauma. In a recent study, 54% of these injuries were received from direct blows to the face, 35% from dropping or throwing incidents, and 8% from violent shaking. In his or her examination of a child following suspected head trauma, the physician will look for injuries to the skull, brain, eyes, ears, nose, and mouth. Whenever there is suspected trauma to the head or face, it is crucial that the child be examined by a physician immediately.

I. The Infant Skull

In the newborn infant, the bones of the skull have not completely formed. At the angles where they do not fully meet, there exist "soft spots" of fibrous tissue called *fontanelles*. When these fontanelles eventually close, they leave sutures which, like immovable joints, separate the bones of the skull. (See Figure 1)

Figure 1

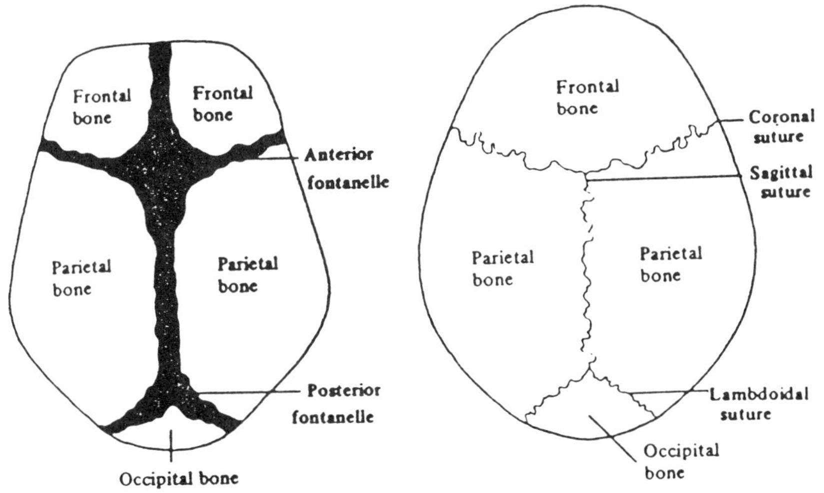

Fontanelles of Infant Skull   Fontanelles of Adult Skull

Introduction to Human Anatomy, 1979
Reprinted with permission

The immaturity of the newborn skull and brain make it more susceptible to trauma. This is because both are more flexible. Because the infant brain floats in a relatively larger space of cerebral fluid than the adult brain, it has more room to move around and sustain injury. Increased pressure from the inside of the skull, either from swelling of the brain or collections of blood, can cause the sutures to separate and bulge.

II. Analysis of Head Injuries

A. Measurement of head circumference

A child having a head circumference measurement over the 90th percentile and/or whose head is growing faster than expected should be examined for intracranial injuries. (See *Appendix D - Growth charts*)

B. Computerized Tomography (CT)

A CT scan is one of the most useful radiographic techniques for detecting acute injuries inside the skull. Whereas a conventional radiography is useful in detecting actual fractures in the skull, the CT scan can detect hemorrhages or subdural hematomas (pockets of blood) which might exist inside the cranium. Use of a CT scan is recommended for infants who, in the presence of suspected trauma, present altered consciousness, retinal hemorrhage, long bone or rib fractures, burns, or excessive bruising. In this situation, a complete skeletal survey may also be recommended.

C. Conventional radiography

Conventional radiography is useful in detecting fractures of the bones in the skull. It is not normally utilized to detect any build-up of fluid. It is important to note that the age of skull fractures generally cannot be estimated.

D. Lumbar spinal tap

Inside the skull, the brain rests suspended inside a pool of fluid which extends from the head into the spinal cord. In a *lumbar spinal tap*, a small amount of this fluid is extracted from the lower portion of the spine. This fluid is part of the fluid which surrounds the brain. The presence of blood in this fluid may signal that bleeding has occurred in some part of this system, most likely in the brain. Occasionally blood from the skin, or from the vessels on the back of the spinal cord, can be in the fluid. This is called a *traumatic spinal tap* and special procedures can be done in the laboratory to determine the origin of the bleeding.

III. Skull Fractures

Skull fractures result when a child receives a direct impact injury to the head. Skull radiology is commonly utilized to detect this type of fracture. Abuse should be suspected when there is no clear history of accidental trauma.

> ## Differential – Accident vs. Abuse
>
> - The best and sometimes the only indicator of the etiology of an injury is the compatibility between the history and the physical findings. Consider the child's developmental maturity. Is he/she capable of performing what the parent or caretaker has reported?
> - A common history given for head injuries is that the child "fell" from a bed, changing table, or sofa. Past studies have suggested, however, that children who fall from heights of 90 cm or less (less than three feet) rarely sustain serious head injury. Although these accidents may cause various bumps, bruises, scratches, etc., those which result in serious injury or fracture should arouse suspicion of abuse. A more recent study of young children confirms that while accidental blunt head injuries are common in young children, they are almost always benign. Severe head trauma is secondary to motor vehicle accidents, falls from *extreme* heights, and inflicted injury by caretakers.

IV. Injury to the Brain

Brain injury can be caused by either direct impact trauma or indirect impact from the Whiplash Shaken Infant Syndrome. This type of trauma is responsible for most of the morbidity and mortality associated with severe head injury. The most common injuries which can occur are:

A. Diffuse cerebral edema

This refers to swelling of the cerebrum, one of the largest portions of the brain. This type of trauma can occur either *laterally* (on one side), or *bilaterally* (on both sides), of the brain. It is the most difficult and life-threatening consequence of head trauma.

B. Infarction

This is a lack of blood to the brain, and can cause *necrosis* (death) of the brain tissue.

C. Cerebral contusions

Cerebral contusions are injuries of the brain tissue caused by direct impact or from the whiplash shaken infant syndrome.

D. Post-traumatic hypopituitarism

This refers to an injury to the pituitary, a part of the brain which secretes hormones affecting growth. This injury, which can result in delayed growth of the child, may be detected through laboratory tests of the hormones.

V. The Whiplash Shaken Infant Syndrome and Subdural Hematoma

A. The Whiplash Shaken Infant Syndrome

In 1972, Dr. John Caffey coined the term "Whiplash Shaken Infant Syndrome" to describe a frequently recognized mechanism of head injury in abused children. This injury involves children who are held by the arms or trunk and severely and repeatedly shaken. Most caretakers are unaware that this type of trauma can cause severe intracranial injuries and even death. The three most common manifestations of this type of abuse are 1) *subdural hematomas*, 2) *retinal hemorrhages*, and 3) *metaphyseal fractures*, a fracture in the growing portion of the bone. (See previous chapter on "Abusive fractures") The brain itself may undergo injury as it is thrown back and forth inside the skull. Bruises on the extremities, or bruising and injury of the thorax (the chest), are often associated findings and support the diagnosis of "shaken infant."

Sometimes children who are victims of the whiplash shaken infant syndrome may also suffer blunt impact to the head. A scenario may be a child who is shaken, then thrown into or against a crib or other surface, striking the back of the head and thus undergoing a large, brief deceleration. This child will have both types of injuries - impact, and severe acceleration-deceleration.

B. Subdural hematoma

Fragile *cerebral veins* bridge the space between the brain and the skull. (See Figure 2) In children, these vessels are poorly supported and can be easily damaged when the head is shaken. Once they are damaged, they release blood into the cavity between the skull and the brain. This blood pools underneath the skull, creating a *subdural hematoma*, which places pressure on the brain tissue. (See Figure 3)

Figure 2

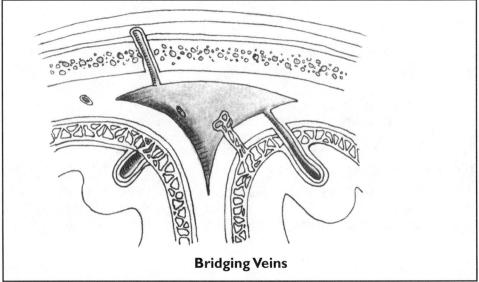

Bridging Veins

Figure 3

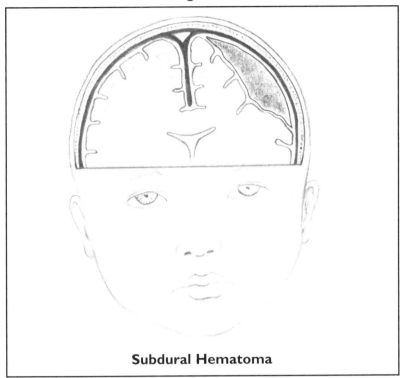

Subdural Hematoma

Acute subdural hematomas occur rapidly following an incident of trauma. *Chronic* subdural hematomas occur slowly, over time, and frequently go undetected. Sometimes both acute and chronic hematomas are present at the same time. These injuries can cause permanent brain damage, seizures, mental retardation, and possibly death. Subdural hematomas can be caused by several different mechanisms, including a heavy moving object striking the head, the moving head striking a heavy stationary object, or the acceleration-deceleration of the Whiplash Shaken Infant Syndrome. Often these injuries occur on both sides of the head, and are frequently accompanied by lethargy, breathing difficulty, convulsions, decreased level of consciousness, vomiting, irritability, retinal hemorrhages and long bone fractures.

CT scans are one of the most useful radiological tools for detecting subdural hematomas. This sensitive form of X-ray can identify collections of fluid around the brain. After identifying a subdural hematoma by CT scan, the physician may, in some cases, choose to "tap" the area of pooled blood with a needle, thus releasing some of the pressure from the brain.

C. Folk practices

The Mexican-American folk remedy for "fallen fontanelle" has been recognized as a cause of subdural hematomas. This practice operates on the mistaken belief that a depression in the top of an infant's skull occurs when the fontanelle, or "soft spot" on the baby's head has "fallen," and can only be retrieved by vigorously sucking the depression back out. Unfortunately, this "remedy" may produce a subdural hematoma. If the parents or caretakers do not respond to counseling and education about these practices, the child may need to be removed from the home.

Differential – Accident vs. Abuse

- Neonates surviving traumatic deliveries such as breech deliveries may sustain serious head injuries, including subdural hematomas. In these cases, the problem should become apparent shortly after birth.
- Benign subdural fluid collection of infancy, or an *effusion*, is another traumatic condition which appears at birth. The CT findings in this condition are different from those in a shake injury; it is also not accompanied by any signs of intracranial injury other than increased head circumference.
- The possibility of child abuse should be seriously considered whenever subdural hematomas are found in an infant or toddler without adequate explanations of trauma.
- *Infectious meningitis* can cause subdural hematomas.

VI. Subgaleal Hematomas and Traumatic Alopecia

Children who have been pulled or yanked by the hair have several common symptoms of this type of abuse. *Traumatic alopecia* is the loss of hair due to some trauma. The hair is often spiraled at the ends where it has stretched and broken off. The scalp may be tender or even bruised at the site where the hair was pulled. *Subgaleal hematomas* occur when the scalp separates from the skull, causing blood to pool under the skin, creating a soft "boggy" area. (See Figure 4) Children with pigtails or braids are often victims of this trauma, for their hair provides accessible "handles" for an angry parent or caretaker.

Differential – Accident vs. Abuse

- A *cephalhematoma*, a swelling under the skin containing blood, may be present on a baby after birth due to passage through the birth canal or if forceps were used in the delivery. This swelling disappears within the first weeks of life.
- *Tinea Capititis* (Ringworm), a fungal infection, may produce round areas of baldness on the scalp. Diagnosis is usually made by fluorescence under a Wood's lamp.

Figure 4

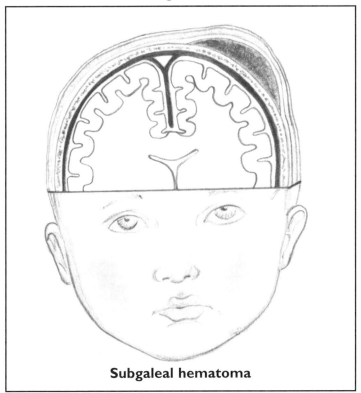

Subgaleal hematoma

VII. Eye Injury

It is estimated that 40% of all child physical abuse cases have some type of ocular problem. These may occur from direct blows to the eyes or from trauma such as the whiplash shake, which leads to retinal hemorrhage. In his or her examination, the physician will usually measure the visual acuity and the field of vision of the eyes.

A. Dislocated lens

Direct blows to the eye may cause the lens to actually detach and become dislocated in the eye. This injury not only affects the child's ability to focus, but also may cause the formation of a *cataract*, or an opacity of the lens. The opthamologist can remove these cataracts in a child, although the child will later need either glasses or contact lenses to correct his or her vision.

B. Subconjunctival hemorrhage

The *conjuctiva* is a mucous membrane which forms the inner surface of the eyelid and covers the front part of the eyeball itself. *Subconjunctival hemorrhage* occurs when a small blood vessel in this membrane breaks, causing the eyeball to appear dark or the lid to appear swollen. These "bruises" usually clear within two weeks; they go through the usual stages of resolution of color from dark red through yellow until they finally disappear.

C. Chemical Burns

Chemical burns to the eye always represent an emergency and should be treated immediately. The eye should always be flushed with water as soon as possible, and the child should be taken to the emergency department of the nearest hospital. Do not overlook the possibility of intentional infliction of chemical injuries as a form of child abuse.

D. Corneal abrasions

The *cornea*, the transparent layer of the front of the eye, should always be checked for lacerations or abrasions following trauma. In treating these cases, the physician will usually protect the eye with a shield to prevent any sort of pressure on the eyeball itself. The child may require tetanus immunization and treatment with antibiotics to treat this injury.

E. Hyphema (accumulation of blood in the eye)

Hyphema refers to a collection of blood in the anterior chamber of the eye, resulting from rupture of blood vessels in that area, most likely from direct trauma to the eye. These injuries are usually treated with topical ointments, although sometimes surgical evacuation of the blood is necessary to help relieve pressure within the eye.

F. Retinal hemorrhage

The *retina* is the delicate innermost layer of the eye. *Retinal hemorrhages* occur as a result of an abrupt increase of pressure in the head (intracranial), or increase of pressure in the chest (intrathoracic). Retinal hemorrhages in abused children are probably secondary to brain trauma, which suddenly increases the pressure within the skull. Whiplash shaken infants often present this condition, as do those sustaining direct impact force to the skull. It is estimated that 50% to 70% of children sustaining subdural hematomas also have retinal hemorrhages. The physician can usually determine this condition by a simple fundoscopic examination, using a special light to examine the retina. Although retinal hemorrhages are not always present in abused children, their presence in conjunction with unexplained fractures, bruises, etc. is a strong indicator that abuse has occurred. It is important that any child who might be a victim of abuse be examined for this common problem.

> **Differential – Accident vs. Abuse**
>
> • Often neonates will exhibit retinal hemorrhages as a result of head trauma sustained during birth. These usually disappear by one month.
> • Because increased pressure on the chest cavity can cause retinal hemorrhages, CPR has, in the past, been questioned as a mechanism producing retinal hemorrhages. It has now been shown that children normally do not receive this type of injury with CPR. When retinal hemorrhage occurs in a child, it should be assumed that the child sustained some type of trauma *before* receiving CPR.

G. Periorbital ecchymosis (bruising around the eyes)

Periorbital ecchymosis, or "black eyes" may be associated with ocular damage. Injury to both eyes should arouse suspicion, for accidental injuries usually occur on one side of the face.

> **Differential – Accident vs. Abuse**
>
> • Allergic conditions can produce bruising under the eyes, the so called "allergic shiners."
> • A documented accidental blow to the forehead or nasal bridge can produce bilateral "black eyes" as blood pools in the loose tissue under the eyes.

VIII. Ear Injury

A. Direct blows

Direct blows to the ear may result in bruising of the *pinna*, the protruding part of the outer ear, perforation of the ear drum, or *hemotympanum*, a collection of blood in the inner ear.

B. Insertion of sharp objects

Lacerations of the external *auditory meatus* (the passage leading from the external to the internal ear), eardrum, or middle or inner ear, can only be achieved by inserting a sharp, pointed object into the ear. These injuries are commonly the result of an adult's innocent attempt to clean a child's ear with cotton swabs. An isolated perforation of the eardrum can occur with infections of the middle ear. The family will usually report the child having ear pain and subsequent draining of pus from the canal. Children with untreated chronically draining ears should be considered at risk for medical neglect.

IX. Nasal Injury

The most common injuries to the nose involve the *nasal septum*, the partition which divides the nasal cavity into two sections. Destruction of the *columella* refers to the part of the septum closest to the tip of the nose. Fractures of the nose are infrequent in the preadolescent years. The insertion of foreign bodies into the nose is a common problem in the normally developing, curious child. Abuse should be suspected when the history does not correspond with the developmental age of the child. Foreign bodies found in more than one site, e.g., nose, ear canals, urogential area, or rectum, should raise stronger suspicions of abuse.

X. Oral Trauma

Its physical significance in both feeding and communication make the mouth an easy target for physical abuse. Injuries to this area include bruises, burns, lesions, "split lips," broken or misplaced teeth, and even fractures of the jaw. The following is a list of common abusive traumas to the mouth.

A. Lacerated frenulum

The *frenula* are the small folds of skin which connect the lips to the gums and connect the tongue to the floor of the mouth. In a recent study, 50% of all nonaccidental injuries involving the head and neck included a torn frenulum of the upper lip. Injuries to this area are very frequent in abuse and should arouse suspicion. The tear can occur from a direct blow to the face or from the jamming of a spoon or bottle into a resistant child's mouth. The latter may be accompanied by bruises of the lips, *palate* (the roof of the mouth), or the *fauces* (the opening leading from the mouth to the throat).

B. Lip injuries

Lip injuries are most often seen as lacerations, bruises, abrasions, and burns. Bruises on the external corners of the mouth indicate the child may have been gagged.

C. Tooth injuries

Traumatic injury to the *deciduous* (baby) teeth of young children are very common. Tooth injuries fall into the following categories: avulsions, fractures, intrusions, and luxations.

1. *Avulsions*

An avulsion refers to a tooth which has been totally removed from the socket. A fairly intense blow is required to cause such an injury. Avulsions require immediate care by a dentist or the tooth will be lost.

2. *Fractures*

Fractures of the teeth can occur from accidental falls or from striking the mouth with a hard instrument. Treatment of these injuries can be performed only by a dentist, and treatment should be sought immediately to avoid losing the tooth.

3. *Intrusion*

Intrusions occur when the teeth are forced into the supporting bone around them. Deciduous teeth are more easily intruded than permanent ones. Teeth will usually re-erupt within three to twelve months.

4. *Luxation*

Teeth that are loosened in the mouth but have not left the socket are referred to as *luxated*. Both deciduous and permanent teeth are easily luxated; the severity of the blow need not be intense for these injuries to occur.

D. Jaw fractures

Fractures of the *maxilla* (upper jaw) are relatively rare in children and are the result of severe trauma. Fractures of the *mandible* (lower jaw) are much more common. Immediate treatment, often by an oral or plastic surgeon, is necessary to avoid disfigurement.

REFERENCES

Bernat, J. (1981). Bite marks and oral manifestations of child abuse and neglect. In N. Ellerstein (Ed.), *Child abuse and neglect: A medical reference.* New York: John Wiley & Sons.

Billmore, E.. & Myers, P. (1985). Serious head injury in infants: accident or abuse? *Pediatrics, 75,* 340.

Duhaime, A.C., et al. (1990). Head injury in very young children: Mechanisms, injury types, and opthalmologic findings in 100 hospitalized patients younger than 2 years of age. *Pediatrics, 90,* 179.

Duhaime, A.C., et al. (1987). The shaken baby syndrome: A clinical, pathological, and biomechanical study. *Journal of Neurosurgery, 66,* 409.

Dykes, L. (1986). The whiplash shaken infant syndrome: What has been learned? *Child Abuse and Neglect, 10,* 211.

Ervin-Mulvey, L., Nelson, L., & Freeley, D. (1983). Pediatric eye trauma. *Pediatric Clinics of North America, 30,* 1167.

Grace, A., & Grace S. (1987). Child abuse within the ear, nose and throat. *The Journal of Otolaryngology, 16,* 108.

Guarnaschelli, F., Lee, J., & Pitts, F.(1972). "Fallen fontanelle" (Caida de Mollera): A variant of the battered child syndrome. *Journal of the American Medical Association, 222,* 1545.

Hahn, Y.L., et al. (1983) Traumatic mechanisms of head injury in child abuse. *Child's Brain, 10,* 229.

Helfer, R.E,. et al. (1977). Injuries resulting when small children fall out of bed. *Pediatrics, 60,* 533.

Kanter, R. (1986). Retinal hemorrhage after cardiopulmonary resuscitation or child abuse. *The Journal of Pediatrics, 108,* 430.

Merten, D., & Osborne, D. (1983). Craniocerebral trauma in the child abuse syndrome. *Pediatric Annals, 12,* 882.

Meservy, C., et al. (1987). Radiographic characteristics of skull fractures resulting from child abuse. *American Journal of Radiology, 149,* 173.

Miller, W., Kaplan, S., & Grumbach, M. (1980). Child abuse as a cause of post-traumatic hypopituitarism. *The New England Journal of Medicine, 302,* 724.

Sinal, S.H., & Ball, M.R. (1987). Head trauma due to child abuse: Serial computerized tomography in dignosis and management. *Southern Medical Journal, 80,* 1505.

Sterne, G., et al. (1986). Oral and dental aspects of child abuse and neglect. *Pediatrics, 78,* 537.

INTERNAL INJURIES

It is estimated that less than 2% of child abuse cases involve *visceral injuries*, injuries to the internal organs. These are extremely serious, however, for when they are present, they have a mortality rate of around 50%. Any blunt trauma to the abdomen or chest involving either a quick, decelerating punch with a fist or object, or involving forceful squeezing, may cause severe damage to the internal organs of a child. We cannot overemphasize the fact that these children need *immediate emergency treatment.*

I. When to Suspect Internal Injuries

If a child has suffered any severe blows to the abdomen, chest, or lower back, he may have incurred internal injuries. Although there are no absolute guidelines for symptoms, the following list details some of the most common indicators that a problem exists.

- Any pain in the stomach, chest, or any internal area.

- External bruising of the chest or stomach.

- Distended or swollen abdomen.

- Tense abdominal muscles.

- Labored breathing.

- Severe pinching pain in the chest while breathing.

- Nausea and/or vomiting.

II. Medical Terminology

Although the doctor treating the child will explain to you the details of the child's particular injuries, the following definitions may be useful to you in understanding the report.

A. Abdominal Injuries

Punches to the abdomen may be especially harmful when directed towards the midline of the body, in which case the organs are pressed against the spine. Abdominal injuries may include any of the following organs.

1. Liver

The liver, the largest organ in the body, serves to filter the blood as it comes from the intestines. These injuries may be referred to as *hepatic injuries*. Of the various abdominal injuries among battered children, these are among the most common. Some injuries may cause the liver to swell, or change shape, while others may actually *lacerate*, or tear, the tissue.

2. *Small Intestine*

The small intestine, a digestive organ attached to the stomach, is composed of three regions, the *duodenum*, the *jejunum*, and the *ileum*. Injuries to this organ are common among abusive abdominal injuries. They may be referred to as *intramural hematomas of the duodenum* or *intramural hematomas of the proximal jejunum*. These terms mean swellings or masses of blood within the walls of the small intestine.

3. *Peritoneum*

This is the membrane which lines the abdominal cavity. Any rupture of this membrane can cause *peritonitis*, inflammation and infection of the peritoneum.

4. *Pancreas*

This gland, situated behind the stomach, produces secretions which aid in digestion. Injuries may produce *pancreatitis*, inflammation of the pancreas, or a *pancreatic pseudocyst*, a cyst-like nodule in the pancreas.

5. *Spleen*

This organ, located in the upper left abdomen, is involved in producing and storing blood. Splenic injuries are one of the most common in nonintentional childhood injuries, for example, bicycle falls.

6. *Kidney*

The kidney filters toxins from the blood, producing urine. (Of *nonintentional* trauma, injuries to the kidney are one of the most common.) Injuries often involve blows to the lower back, and are frequently accompanied by pain to that area.

B. *Thoracic (Chest) Injuries*

Injuries to the chest are dangerous because broken ribs can puncture or damage the lungs, causing a *pneumothorax*, a collection of air in the pleural cavity, which is the sac-enclosed area surrounding the lungs. A *hemothorax* refers to blood fluid in the pleural cavity caused by ruptured vessels. *Pulmonary contusions* are any bruises to the lungs.

III. Assessment

In his initial assessment, the doctor will palpate the abdomen, feeling for any unusual swelling, tenderness, or rigidity. Some of the possible tests are: blood tests or radiographic tests (X-rays); *urography*, radiography of the urinary tract; *ultrasonography*, the use of ultrasound to produce images of organs or tissues; *CAT Scan,* a form of radiography, or *angiography,* radiography of the blood vessels.

IV. Treatment

Any cases in which abdominal trauma is suspected require immediate referral; the earlier they are detected, the better the chances of the child's survival. Nevertheless, an estimated number of these injuries will result in death. Treatments for individual injuries will vary with each particular case; almost all will require a hospital stay. Children who experience shock due to blood loss may also experience central nervous system problems.

REFERENCES

Gornall, P., Ahmed, S., Jolleys, A., & Cohen, D.J. (1972). Intra-abdominal injuries in the battered baby syndrome. *Archives of Diseases in Childhood, 47,* 211.

Jewett, T.C. (1981) Chest and abdominal injuries. In N. Ellerstein (Ed.), *Child abuse and neglect: A medical reference.* New York:John Wiley & Sons.

Kirks, D. (1983). Radiological evaluation of visceral injuries. *Pediatric Annals, 12,* 888.

Kleinman, P.K., Brill, P.W., & Winchester, P. (1986). Resolving duodenal-jejunal hematoma in abused children. *Radiology, 160,* 747.

CHILD ABUSE BY POISONING

Dr. C. Henry Kempe first referred to poisoning as a form of child abuse in 1962. Since that date, workers in both the medical and CPS fields have become increasingly aware of this and other less obvious forms of abuse. In a recent review of the literature on nonaccidental poisoning, it was found that 17% of the reported cases resulted in mortality. Twenty percent of the cases reviewed were also related to physical abuse. Dr. Ronald Fischler divides nonaccidental poisoning into four distinct categories: 1) impulsive acts under stress; 2) bizarre child-rearing practices; 3) neglect (lack of supervision); and 4) Munchausen's Syndrome by Proxy. With increased reporting, the patterns of these four categories are becoming more and more clearly defined.

I. Impulsive Acts Under Stress

It is not surprising that the same stressful environment which might invoke a parent or caretaker to hit a child might also invoke him to give drugs to a child. Drug administration with the intent to sedate is in fact probably the most common reason for nonaccidental poisoning. Sedatives such as alcohol, barbiturates, or antihistamines are most commonly used in this practice. Parents may use drugs which have been prescribed for themselves or they may use those prescribed by a pediatrician, most likely for colic.

When this problem is recognized early and when the family is capable of learning the hazards of medication in children, the results of appropriate intervention are usually good. When parents or caretakers are under continually high stress, are unable to change their behavior, or are drug abusers themselves, the option of removing the child from the home should be considered.

II. Bizarre Child-Rearing Practices

Parents or caretakers who poison their children by adhering to bizarre child-rearing practices fall into two categories: those who are well-intentioned yet uneducated, and those who intentionally use poisoning as a form of punishment.

A. Nonintentional poisoning

Some parents or caretakers may accidentally poison their children by giving them toxic doses of vitamins, minerals, herbs, or "roots," in an attempt to cure an illness or to ward off disease. Alternatively, a parent might feed a baby an improperly diluted formula, resulting in either water or salt intoxication. Although these mistakes are forms of neglect which should be reported, they are often successfully treated with education, support, and a close monitoring of the situation.

B. Poisoning as a form of punishment

Parents or caretakers may wish to punish children by forcing them to ingest toxic amounts of chemicals or food. Others may give their children drugs to initiate them into the drug culture. Both practices can cause severe damage to the child, both physically and psychologically. If you are aware that a child has been repetitively forced to ingest any substance as a form of punishment, or if he or she suffers adverse effects from even one episode, you should have the child examined by a doctor. The following list includes substances reported in this type of abuse:

1. Table salt
Frequently used as a punishment for bed-wetting, the forced ingestion of table salt is the most common form of nonaccidental poisoning. The resulting *hypernatremia*, excess sodium in the blood, causes dehydration, seizures, and vomiting.

2. Water intoxication
The second most frequently reported form of abuse, also a common punishment for enuresis (involuntary urination), is the forced ingestion of water. The resulting *hyponatremia*, a decreased amount of sodium in the blood, is among the most common pediatric electrolytic disorders. This condition can lead to seizures, convulsions, confusion, lethargy, and comas. Other causes for this condition are metabolic disorders and inappropriate use of baby formula.

3. Hot peppers or "Texas Pete"
The forced ingestion of hot peppers and their derivatives can damage the mucous membranes of the mouth and stomach as well as injure the nervous system. These can also become clogged in the child's throat, leading to problems in breathing.

4. Ground black pepper
The powdered consistency of ground black pepper can cause it to become clogged in the throat or lungs, leading to *apnea*, cessation of breathing.

5. Laxatives
Excessive ingestion of laxatives and the resulting diarrhea may lead to severe dehydration, fever, and bloody stools.

6. Household products
Various substances reported in this type of abuse are lye derivatives (toilet bowl cleaner), hydrocarbons (lighter fluid), detergents, and oil.

7. Drugs
Drugs reported in abusive ingestion include anticoagulants (blood thinners), insulin, barbiturates, quaaludes, antidepressants, sedatives, tranquilizers, and pain killers.

III. Neglect (lack of supervision)

Most accidental poisonings are the result of improper storage of household chemicals such as bleach, charcoal, lighter fluid, furniture polish, or kerosene. In most cases, the parents or caretakers are concerned and seek medical attention promptly. These cases can usually be managed by educating the parents or caretakers on home safety. Repeated accidental poisoning may indicate outright neglect or stress within the family. Other signals, such as uncleanliness, malnourishment, or lack of medical care may also indicate neglect. These cases should be assessed for neglect and possible physical abuse.

IV. Munchausen's Syndrome by Proxy (MSP)

This increasingly reported form of abuse is one of the most misleading and hard to diagnose. The next section discusses this parenting disorder in detail.

V. Assessment and Management

In the assessment and management of suspected poisoning, the physician and CPS worker must work together in gathering and documenting a complete medical and social history. The former should include all previous poisoning episodes. The social history should include:

- Parent/caretaker occupation(s).

- Unusual illnesses/hospital admissions of siblings.

- History of previous illness of parents/caretakers or family (psychiatric, drug/alcohol abuse, underlying disease).

- A list of all drugs available to the parents and in the child's surroundings.

Keep in mind that no "toxicology screens" are truly comprehensive. Toxicology testing in a particular institution usually reflects the incidence with which a toxin is encountered in that geographical area. Therefore, the social history is imperative to the selection of appropriate tests.

REFERENCES

Baugh, J., Krug, E.., & Weir, M. (1993). Punishment by salt poisoning. *Southern Medical Journal, 76,* 540.

Cross, R. (1992). Toxicology testing: What you get may not be what you requested (or needed). *Bulletin of Laboratory Medicine, The University of North Carolina Hospitals, 126.*

Dine, M., & McGovern, M. (1982). Intentional poisoning of children - an overlooked category of child abuse: Report of seven cases and review of the literature. *Pediatrics, 70,* 32.

Fischler, R. (1983). Poisoning: a syndrome of child abuse. *American Family Physician, 28,* 103.

Rogers, D., et al., (1976). Non-accidental poisoning: An extended syndrome of child abuse. *British Medical Journal, 1,* 703.

Saulsbury, F., Chobanion, M., & Wilson, W. (1984). Child abuse: Parental hydrocarbon administration. *Pediatrics, 73,* 719.

Tilelli, J., & Ophoven, J. (1986). Hyponatremic seizures as a presenting symptom of child abuse. *Forensic Science International, 30,* 213.

Tominack, R., & Spyker, D. (1987). Capsicum and capsiacin - A review: Case report of the use of hot peppers in child abuse. *Clinical Toxicology, 25,* 591.

Zahavi, I., Shaffer, E.A., & Gall, D.G. (1982). Child abuse with laxatives. *Canadian Medical Association Journal, 127,* 512.

Munchausen's Syndrome by Proxy

I. Definition

Munchausen's syndrome by proxy (MSP) is an abusive parenting disorder still highly unrecognized by both the medical and nonmedical professionals. The syndrome derives its name from the eighteenth century Baron Karl Frederick von Munchausen, who wrote a book of wild, exaggerated tales of his life's adventures. In 1951, the term Munchausen's syndrome was used to describe adults who produce false medical histories and fabricate physical symptoms and laboratory findings, causing themselves needless medical tests and evaluations, sometimes even surgery.

Consequently, in 1977, Dr. Roy Meadow created the term "Munchausen's syndrome by proxy" to describe a form of child abuse in which the parent or caretaker relates fictitious illnesses in his or her child by either inducing or fabricating the signs or symptoms. As a result, the child is subjected to extensive medical tests and hospitalization. The technical definition of MSP includes:

1) An illness in a child which is faked and/or produced by a parent or caretaker.

2) A parent or parent figure who presents the child for medical care persistently, often resulting in multiple medical procedures.

3) Denial of knowledge by perpetrator as to the etiology of the illness.

4) Acute symptoms which abate when the child is separated from the parent/caretaker.

It is estimated that nine percent of all recognized MSP cases have resulted in mortality. All of these deaths occurred in children under three years of age.

II. Case History

A six-month-old infant was repeatedly brought to the hospital by a parent for seizures and apnea spells (lack of breathing). Electro-encephalograms (EEG's) and the medical examination were normal on multiple occasions. No seizures or apnea were ever noted by health care personnel. On a number of occasions, immediately after discharge from the hospital, or after a clinic visit, the child was brought to the hospital by ambulance for another spell. The child was hospitalized in a special room with a constantly recording EEG and a videotape of the child. On two occasions, the EEG showed abnormalities while the parent held the child out of range of the camera. The EEG machine broke and was removed from the room while the videotape machine was left running, unknown to the parent. Later the same day, the parent came out of the room and called the nurse because the baby had "stopped breathing." A review of the videotape suggested that the parent had held a pillow over the baby's face prior to calling the nurse.

III. Characteristics of MSP

A. The victim

Boys and girls stand an equal chance of becoming victims of MSP. Although infants and toddlers are at the age of highest victimization, cases have been reported in older children. Two medical problems which frequently accompany MSP are failure-to-thrive (FTT), and iron deficiency anemia. A child may develop an actual illness as a result of his or her subjection to the parent's treatment or as a result of the invasive investigation of the medical staff. The legitimate existence of a disease should not exclude the child from the possible diagnosis of MSP.

B. The parents/caretakers

In all of the cases of MSP documented in the literature prior to 1990, the perpetrator has been the mother or foster mother of the victim. The father is often distant and uninvolved with the family. Often he appears completely unaware of the problem that exists. The mothers are frequently:

- Intelligent and articulate, with friendly, socially adept personalities.

- Capable of forming a close but "shallow" rapport with the hospital staff.

- Extremely close and attentive of the child, claiming that child will eat or take medication "only for her."

- Isolated and emotionally distant from their husbands, families, and friends.

- Medically knowledgeable, to some degree.

Although psychological and psychiatric treatment is always recommended for these mothers, the treatment in documented cases has rarely been successful and fails to produce any diagnostic label for her condition. The most common condition which has been recognized is depression.

The initial published case of a father as perpetrator involves an infant admitted six times for reported apnea, reported apnea with seizures, and finally reported blood in the mouth and stool added to the previous complaints. On the last admission, apneic spells and tremors occurred for the first time during hospitalization. On the third day postadmission, the father was discovered pressing the infant's face against the crib mattress. This case nicely illustrates a phenomenon previously noted in mother perpetrator cases, that is, the escalation of reported and/or produced symptoms over time; however, this particular father does not fit the profile previously described in mothers. The parents were young, unwed, and unemployed; the father was not overly friendly to the staff, at times accusing them of not knowing what was going on with his infant, and expressing frustration at the lack of answers. Whether the prevalence of father figures as perpetrators of MSP is more common than previously suspected and whether the characteristics of father perpetrators are different are currently unanswered questions.

C. Signs of MSP

Adapted from the work of Dr. G. Jones, et al. (1996).

1) Recurrent or persistent illnesses for which a cause cannot be found.

2) History and physical findings do not coincide.

3) Symptoms do not occur when the child is away from the mother.

4) Unusual symptoms, signs, or hospital course that do not make clinical sense.

5) A differential diagnosis consisting of disorders less common than Munchausen's syndrome by proxy.

6) Child fails to tolerate or respond to medical therapy without clear cause.

7) A parent/caretaker less concerned than the physician, sometimes comforting the medical staff.

8) Repeated hospitalizations and vigorous medical evaluations of mother or child.

9) A parent/caretaker who is constantly at the child's bedside, excessively praises the staff, becomes overly attached to the staff, or becomes highly involved in the care of other patients.

10) A parent/caretaker who welcomes or requests medical tests of her child, even when painful.

D. Commonly simulated and produced illnesses of MSP

Simulated illnesses are fictitious, while *produced* illnesses are those whose symptoms really do exist. An example of the latter would be a child presenting with chronic diarrhea produced by unnatural causes, such as poisoning with laxatives. The following list of symptoms are those commonly seen in MSP (Rosenberg, 1987).

Presentation	Method of simulation and/or production
Bleeding	-Drug poisoning -Application of exogenous blood to diapers or laboratory specimens. (For example, the mother putting her own menstrual blood into the child's urine specimen.) -Addition of other substances, such as paint, cocoa or dyes to clothes.
Seizures	-Lying -Drug poisoning -Suffocation
Central Nervous System Depression	-Drug poisoning -Suffocation
Apnea (cessation of breathing)	-Lying -Drug poisoning -Suffocation
Diarrhea	-Lying -Drug poisoning
Vomiting	-Lying -Drug poisoning -Induced
Fever	-Falsifying temperature -Falsifying chart
Rash	-Drug poisoning -Scratching or rubbing the skin -Caustics applied to the skin.
Polymicrobial Bacteremia (bacteria in the blood)	-Addition of contaminants to the the blood. (For example, injecting fecal material into a child's IV line that goes directly into the blood.)

IV. Treatment

A. General guidelines

Dr. Roy Meadow suggests the following guidelines for the course of treatment of MSP.

1. Separate the child from the mother to see if there is an occurrence of symptoms and signs in her absence.

2. Obtain detailed family psychosocial history and check its veracity. The mother's medical history should be examined for fabricated symptoms of her own, and to determine whether the mother has donated the child symptoms of her own history.

3. Check the temporal relationship between symptoms, signs, and presence of the mother.

4. Keep specimens collected on admission and during the recurrence of symptoms for detailed investigation.

5. Repeatedly check the reliability of the signs. (Is it really blood? Is it the child's blood?)

6. Enroll psychiatric help.

B. Role of the physician and social worker

1. Physician
The primary care physician should be responsible for the collection and review of all pertinent medical records of both the child and mother. He should work closely with the CPS worker in making recommendations regarding placement.

2. CPS Worker

a. *History*
The CPS worker should obtain a social history of the child, the mother/caretaker, and the immediate family. These histories should be verified, since they are often fabricated by the mother. The history should include:

• Any unusual illness or hospital admission of siblings.

• Previous illness of the parent/caretakers.

• A list of all drugs available to the parent.

In addition to the social history, the CPS worker may need to help the physician in the collection of medical records, as this can often be a lengthy, time-consuming process.

b. *Recommendations regarding placement*
In the decisions regarding placement of the child, the CPS/medical team will need to closely consider each particular case. Often an initial removal of the child will allow time to assess the parents/caretakers and to appraise the success of initial intervention. It is recommended that children not return to the home if the mother is unresponsive to treatment, or denies the problem entirely. Placement in the home of the mother, but under the father's supervision, is not considered a safe alternative.

C. Obstacles in the treatment of MSP

1. Lack of knowledge
One of the largest roadblocks to treatment of these cases is the public's lack of knowledge of MSP. Both the physician and CPS worker will need to educate others, such as attorneys and the courts, about this form of child abuse.

2. Disbelief
Often the parents will befriend the medical staff, CPS staff, attorneys, and courts. Their attempts to "charm" people into believing their innocence are often successful, and thus a hindrance in the treatment of MSP. Also, courts tend to rely heavily on psychiatric evaluations. In the past, these have proven fairly ineffectual in diagnosing mental deficiencies in MSP mothers.

3. Doctor shopping
In their constant search for sympathy from the medical profession, mother/caretakers will often "Doctor Shop," moving from hospital to hospital, sometimes even leaving the state to do so. The scattered locations of these professionals often make the collections of medical records and histories a laborious, lengthy process.

REFERENCES

Jones, G., et al. (1996). Munchausen syndrome by proxy. *Child Abuse & Neglect, 10,* 33.

Makar, A., & Squier, P. (1990). Munchausen syndrome by proxy: Father as a perpetrator. *Pediatrics, 85,* 370.

Meadow, R. (1977). Munchausen syndrome by proxy: The hinterland of child abuse. *Lancet 2,* 343.

Rosenberg, D. (1987). Web of deceit: A literature review of Munchausen syndrome by proxy. *Child Abuse & Neglect, 11,* 547.

Woollcott, P., et al. (1982). Doctor shopping with the child as proxy patient: A variant of child abuse. *The Journal of Pediatrics, 101,* 297.

Zitelli, B., Seltman, M., & Shannon, R. (1987). Munchausen's syndrome by proxy and its professional participants. *American Journal of Diseases of Childhood, 141,* 1099.

CHILD SEXUAL ABUSE

American Humane Association • Children's Division • Understanding the Medical Diagnosis of Child Maltreatment

CHILD SEXUAL ABUSE

In most states the legal definition for the molestation of a child is an act of a person, adult or child, which forces, coerces, or threatens a child to have any form of sexual contact or to engage in any type of sexual activity at his or her direction. This includes inappropriate touching (clothed or unclothed); penetration using an object; forcing sexual activity between children; or asking a child to view, to read, or to pose for pornographic materials. The incidence of child sexual abuse reports has increased significantly since 1980, in some areas up to three times the previous level. North Carolina's Division of Social Services substantiated 1,500 cases of sexual abuse in '92-'93, which was a 22% increase from the previous year.

It is impossible to overemphasize the importance of a thorough physical and genital exam in suspected cases of sexual abuse. When a child shows either behavioral or physical symptoms of sexual abuse, he or she should receive a complete physical and genital exam from a skilled examiner. Many parents and caretakers do not realize that the pediatric gynecological exam is very different from that performed on adults. In fact, only in rare cases will the experienced physician actually use a speculum in the examination.

As with all medical evaluations, the complete history is one of the most important components of a medical examination for sexual abuse. This history includes the presenting problem and symptoms, past medical history, developmental history, and family history. The history is crucial for the physician to understand the course of symptoms, and to clarify other conditions which may be confused with sexual abuse. The physical examination is most helpful when it is complete, that is a "head-to-toe" exam, and when it is done with a thorough history. This approach helps the physician to find links between the history and the physical, and to form a more complete differential diagnosis.

The medical examination in sexual abuse has several purposes.

Purposes of Medical Exam
- Identify conditions requiring urgent treatment.
- Examine the whole body for any abnormalities and assess pubertal development
- Obtain physical evidence if present.
- Reassure the child and family of physical intactness and/or healing.
- Facilitate the child or adolescent's regaining control of his/her body.
- Formulate a plan for treatment recommendations.

I. When to Seek an Exam for Sexual Abuse

The first important decision which you must make involving suspected cases of abuse is determining when to have a physician examine the child. If the abuse has occurred within the past 72 hours, he or she should be examined immediately for the purpose of collecting data or specimens crucial in legal proceedings, and because healing can be very rapid. In other cases, the immediate exam is not as urgent as beginning the history and preparing the family and child for the exam. Use these general guidelines in your decision.

- If the abuse occurred or may have occurred within the past 72 hours, the child should be seen immediately. It has been estimated that non-motile sperm may be detected for up to three days following ejaculation. Preferably, the child should not bathe, change clothes, or use the bathroom before the examination.

- If the child has vaginal pain; bleeding or discharge from the urethra, vagina, or rectum; painful urination (dysuria); or complains of pain when walking or sitting, the physician should be seen immediately.

- Children who have been abused weeks or months previously should be examined as soon as it is practical, preferably within a few days.

- Siblings of suspected victims of sexual abuse should also be examined as soon as practical. (Muram, 1991)

- Children with repeated complaints of abdominal pain or vaginal inflammation with no other symptoms should be considered as possible abuse victims and examined as soon as it is practical.

II. Behavioral Changes Indicating Abuse

The first indicators of sexual abuse may not be physical signs, but behavioral changes or abnormalities. Unfortunately, adults around the child may misinterpret these signals as disobedience or impudence on the part of the child.

A. Normal child sexual development

Before you can identify any behavior as abnormal, it is important to become familiar with the normal sexual development, related behaviors, interactions and feelings of the growing child. The following summary, adapted from Hillman and Solek-Tefft's **Spiders and Flies**, gives not only "normal" behaviors in childhood development, but common "abnormal" behaviors which may indicate abuse. It is important to remember that no child will follow these developmental stages exactly. Some may mature more quickly, others more slowly, and others may have different behaviors occurring naturally from the influence of their particular environment. Deviations in behavior do not necessarily indicate a serious problem, or sexual abuse in particular, but should be assessed in the context of the history, physical findings, and the child's family environment.

1. Infancy (birth to one year)
This stage includes three phases of psychosexual development.

a. Pair bonding
Sometimes called the oral stage of development, in the early phase the child derives pleasure and security from sucking, body contact, cuddling, rocking movements, clinging, and touching. Genital touching may occur naturally here, as infants enjoy touching all parts of their body randomly.

b. Genital play
Genital self-touching usually occurs between the ages of six and twelve months as a part of the child's exploration of his own body. Although it usually begins during the third year, masturbation might occur in the first two years. Infants may thrust their pelvis when being cuddled or falling asleep. This behavior should diminish over time. It is important that the parents/caretaker do not punish the infant for self-stimulation or masturbation.

c. Identification of gender, or sex role
This stage of development determines how the parent will bring up the child. Having an assigned gender role will help the child identify with the same sex parent and with socially approved sex role behaviors and standards. Occasionally this is not the same as his or her biological sex.

Behavioral Symptoms of Sexual Abuse
- Displacing of fear and anxiety through excessive crying and fretful behavior.
- Physical ailments such as vomiting, feeding problems, bowel disturbances, and sleep problems.
- Failure to thrive.

---

2. Toddler and Early Childhood (two to five years)
Toilet training, with all of the pressures and anxieties involved, usually occurs during this stage, referred to as the *anal stage*. Common sexual behaviors observed in three-year-olds include handling of their own genitals, kissing parents and other children, cuddling, and a beginning awareness of genital differences between males and females.

As children enter early childhood they usually enter the *phallic stage*, in which directed genital play and specific sexual sensations and feelings are first manifested. Common sexual behavior at age four includes kissing, cuddling, touching, and mild masturbation. The child may show an increased curiosity about sex. At this stage, they may purposely display their genitals to peers. They are often fascinated by excretion. At the same time, children begin to develop a need for increased privacy, especially in the bathroom.

Five-year-olds are usually more serious, self-contained, and better able to imitate adult behavior. Open genital display decreases, as well as bathroom fascination. Children play interpersonal games, including family, marriage, doctor, and store.

Behavioral Symptoms of Sexual Abuse
• Fear of a particular person or place.
• Regression to earlier forms of behavior such as bed-wetting, stranger anxiety, separation anxiety, thumb-sucking, baby talk, whining, and clinging.
• Victimization of others.
• Fear of being abandoned if the caretaker cannot come to the child's assistance or momentarily leaves.
• Feelings of strong shame or guilt.
• Excessive masturbation.

---

3. Latency (six to nine years)
Six-year-olds have an increased awareness of, and interest in, the anatomical differences between sexes. They may ask practical questions about sex, such as how a baby comes out of the mother's stomach and if it hurts the mother in the process. Children at this age think of marrying someone of the opposite sex.

Seven-year-olds are still quite interested in the topic of birth. Children are often discrete about their bodies and more anxious about being touched. Children may talk and joke about boyfriends and girlfriends. Occasional masturbation is common. Intense or frequent masturbation may signal anxiety, distress, or sexual abuse.

At the ages of eight and nine, children display increased secretive behavior among peers and an increased interest in socialization. Specific sexual interest remains diffuse, and sexual behavior is often absent or discrete.

> ### Behavioral Symptoms of Sexual Abuse
> - Nightmares and other sleep disturbances.
> - Fear that the attack will recur.
> - Phobias concerning specific school or community activities or specific people.
> - Withdrawal from family and friends.
> - Regression to earlier behaviors.
> - Eating disturbances.
> - Physical ailments such as abdominal pain or urinary difficulties.

4. Preadolescence (ten to twelve years)

Initial signs of puberty and the development of secondary sexual characteristics occur at this stage. Strong friendships as well as budding romances occur at this stage. Boys and girls may engage in playful tickling or hitting which, although it may have some degree of sexuality, does not seem directly motivated by sexual concerns.

> ### Behavioral Symptoms of Sexual Abuse
> - Depression.
> - Nightmares and other sleep disturbances.
> - Poor school performance.
> - Promiscuity.
> - Use of illegal drugs or alcohol.
> - Fear that the attack will recur.
> - Eating disturbances.
> - Regression to earlier behaviors.
> - Withdrawal from family and friends.
> - Aggression.

5. Early Adolescence (thirteen to fifteen years)

This stage is characterized by two major changes: pubertal maturation and interest in peer group involvement. Girls usually begin menstruation by this period, and boys experience ejaculation through dreams or fondling. Both experience strong sexual feelings, with sexual dreams and fantasies. Interest in adult movies and reading material develops. Masturbation is common at this stage.

Behavioral Symptoms of Sexual Abuse

- Running away from home.
- Severe depression.
- Early marriage.
- Promiscuity (sometimes to the point of prostitution).
- Early pregnancy.
- Use of illegal drugs or alcohol.
- Suicidal thoughts or gestures.
- School truancy.
- Poor school performance.
- Pronounced fear that the attack will recur.
- Grief over the loss of one's virginity.
- Anger and rage about being forced into a situation beyond one's control.
- Withdrawal from family and friends.
- Pseudomature behaviors.

6. Adolescence (sixteen to twenty years)

Adolescent boys and girls begin assuming adult roles at this stage. Their desire to be independent may cause conflicts and family problems. They may purposely violate sexual restrictions to gain distance from family problems and to release tension. Serious problems of unchecked sexuality may occur at this stage, such as out-of-wedlock pregnancy, abortion, or venereal disease. In this stage, sexual abuse is similar to rape in that it can occur in individuals who have had sexual intercourse of their own accord.

B. The Child Sexual Abuse Accommodation Syndrome

From his experiences working with sexually abused children, Dr. Roland Summit recognized five common characteristics among childhood sexual abuse victims. In 1983, he categorized these into what he calls the "Child Abuse Accommodation Syndrome." You should be aware of these five classic stages frequently encountered in sexually abused children.

1. Secrecy

In order for prolonged sexual abuse to occur, the perpetrator must establish some form of secrecy with the child. Often this secrecy relies on threats or illogical explanations of why the child should not tell of the abuse. No matter how sincere or gentle these explanations may seem, their implied danger and secrecy make it clear to the child that his/her acts are something bad and dangerous. Most children never tell their secret. Often, when it is uncovered, adults fail to comprehend the fear which has caused the child to remain silent for so long. They react with anger and disbelief, wondering why the child did not tell sooner, or why he or she wanted to keep it a secret for so long.

2. Helplessness

In their consideration of abuse, many adults fail to realize the helpless position of the child who often depends on the perpetrator for food, shelter, and basic family security. Adults may assume that the child who does not complain is, in a sense, consenting to the relationship, when in reality, he/she has no choice. They expect the child to cry for help, struggle to escape, and resist. With most children, however, this is not the case. Even when the perpetrator is not a caretaker, the child may feel powerless to refuse an adult's requests.

3. Entrapment and accommodation

Sexual molestation is often not a one-time occurrence. Frequently these relationships develop into addictive, compulsive patterns which continue until the child either leaves home or the situation is discovered. In order to deal with this continuous fear and subjection, most children have no choice but to submit to their situations. "The only healthy option left for the child is to learn to accept the situations and to survive . . . The healthy, normal, emotionally resilient child will learn to accommodate to the reality of continuing sexual abuse" (Summit, 1983). Often this accommodation involves self-punishment and self-blame, depression, and guilt. He or she may create imaginary companions or even develop multiple personalities. Some children become aggressive and show outward rage. Others may turn to substance abuse. All of these behaviors are part of the child's "survival skills." They can only be overcome if the child can finally gain trust in a secure environment which provides consistent acceptance and care.

4. Delayed, conflicted, and unconvincing disclosure

As the abused child begins to mature into adolescence, he or she experiences a new sense of independence. At this point, the accommodation syndrome breaks down. Sometimes a family conflict or discovery by another person may trigger the breakdown. As the child's self-made walls of protection begin to crumble, the victim begins to rebel against the family's protectiveness. He or she may choose friends they do not like, drink, abuse drugs, break the law, or run away. Unfortunately, it is not until the victim reaches this stage of rebelliousness that he/she decides to tell the secret. Under these conditions, however, the disclosures go unheeded. "Authorities are alienated by the pattern of delinquency and rebellious anger . . . Most adults . . . tend to identify with the problems of parents in trying to cope with a rebellious teenager" (Summit, 1983). Mothers as well, typically react with disbelief and denial. The paradox of the disclosure of sexual abuse is that it is not until the child has become rebellious that he or she has the courage to tell the secret. By then, however, the prosecution does not accept the victim as a reliable witness, for he or she is hardly considered sweet and innocent anymore.

5. Retraction

Once a child has told that he or she has been molested, the fears and threats underlying the secrecy become true. The victim's mother rejects the child; the father calls the child a liar. The father may be arrested or have to move out of the home. Under these circumstances, most children reverse their story, denying that it ever happened and "admitting" that it was made up. "Unless trained specialists take immediate intervention to force responsibility on the father, the girl will follow the 'normal' course and retract her complaint." (Summit, 1983)

III. Presenting the Child for Examination

It is important that you alert the doctor to any clues in the history which might lead to specific evidence in the following areas. Try to include as many of the following pieces of information as possible when you are relating the history to the doctor.

- Why do you think that this child has been abused? Has the child reported genital or anal pain? Has she had any discharge? Has the child's behavior been abnormal?

- How exactly was the child abused? Was there genital, anal, or oral contact?

- When exactly was the last incidence of suspected abuse? How long has the abuse been going on? Has this child or anyone in his or her environment been examined for sexual abuse?

- If the child is an adolescent, might he or she be sexually active?

- Is there anyone that you know of in the family's living environment who has, or has had in the past, a sexually transmitted disease?

- Has the child ever been examined for any type of physical abuse or neglect?

- Does the child masturbate? If so, is he or she punished for doing so? How is the child punished?

- Is the parent/caretaker applying any ointments or creams to the child's genitals?

- Is there any history of genital surgery or documented accidental trauma?

When a child presents vaginal or anal irritation as a reason for suspected abuse, you should help the doctor investigate for other possibilities which might cause the problem. Discuss with the parent other causes of irritation, such as:

- Could the child be reacting allergically to any new bathing soaps, bubble baths, or clothing detergents?

- Has the child recently had any other infections or illnesses? Has the child been taking any antibiotics?

- How would you describe the discharge? (color, foul-smelling, copious)

- Is the child toilet-trained?

- How often is the child bathed? How often are the child's diapers changed?

- Does the child wear any type of clothing, such as tight jeans, plastic covered paper diapers, or sanitary pads, which might cause irritation?

IV. The Physical Exam

Depending on the age of the child and the circumstances of the abuse, he or she may wish to have you, or perhaps the mother, remain in the examining room. Your presence will not only help calm the child, but will also allow you to hear first hand the physician's interview and learn of any immediate findings. This may help you to understand the physical aspects of the case more clearly.

Do not expect to leave the initial examination knowing for certain if a child has or has not been abused. Although in some cases it is obvious immediately, the majority of sexually molested children younger than ten years of age have normal findings on their genital exams. A normal physical and negative culture results should not exclude the possibility of sexual abuse.

The physician will begin with a general physical examination of the child, checking the body for bruises, swellings, abrasions, lacerations, or bite marks. This initial part of the exam not only de-emphasizes the genital exam, but may also provide evidence of physical abuse or neglect which may aid in later legal proceedings. For this purpose, photographs may be taken of any existing trauma.

The physician will strive to make the genital exam as nontraumatic as possible, by taking plenty of time to explain each step of the examination, how it will feel, and what will be done. The doctor may ask the child to "show where it hurts" or "where the peepee comes out." In some cases in which the child seems excessively fearful of the exam, or has already been dramatically traumatized, the physician may not be able to reassure the child and may choose to sedate the child. This procedure allows the completion of a thorough exam without adding to the child's traumatic experience.

A. Genital Assessment

Most of the genital assessment involves a clear, careful, external examination. The young female is often most comfortable when examined on the exam table or seated in someone's lap, lying on her back with her heels drawn up to the buttocks and knees apart (the "frog leg" position). Another position is the "knee-chest" position, in which the child rests her head on her folded arms and supports her weight on her bent knees. The "knee chest" position is used to examine the anus as well as the hymenal area. The "dorsal lithotomy" position, which may be used for adolescent exams, describes the position using stirrups, familiar as the adult pelvic position. There are various techniques (separation and traction) for holding the genital labia apart to visualize the hymen and surrounding areas. In his assessment, the physician will examine the vagina as well as the anus for signs of old and new trauma and for hygiene. He will assess the condition of the hymen as well as the size of the hymenal ring and the vaginal introitus (the vaginal opening). Frequently, he will refer to the positions of specific findings as on the face of a clock, as indicated in Figure 1.

In his physical exam the physician will assess the child's physical sexual maturity. Because all children develop at different ages, physicians refer to one common index, from which they can rank the stage of each particular child's development on a scale of one to five (I-V). These stages are classified as Tanner stages. (See Table 1)

Figure I

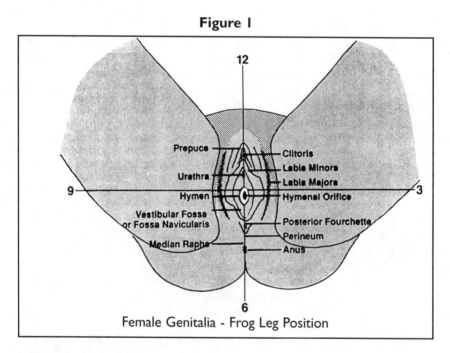

Female Genitalia - Frog Leg Position

1. Female genitalia

Clitoris — the highly sensitive, erectile organ of the female vulva.

Hymen — the mucous membrane which partially surrounds the vaginal opening. See below for detail.

Table I

Tanner Stages

Classification of Sexual Maturity Stages in Girls		Classification of Sexual Maturity Stages in Boys	
Stage I		**Stage I**	
Pubic Hair	Preadolescent	Pubic Hair	None
Breasts	Preadolescent	Penis	Preadolescent
		Testes	Preadolescent
Stage II		**Stage II**	
Pubic Hair	Sparse, slightly pigmented (darkened), straight, at (middle) border of labia	Pubic Hair	Scanty, long, slightly pigmented.
Breasts	Breast and papilla (nipple) elevated as small mound, areolar(pigmented area) diameter increased	Penis	Slight enlargement
		Testes	Enlarged scrotum, pink, texture changed
Stage III		**Stage III**	
Pubic Hair	Darker, beginning to curl, increased amount	Pubic Hair	Darker, begins to curl, small amount
Breasts	Breast and areola enlarged, without contour separation	Penis	Longer
		Testes	Larger
Stage IV		**Stage IV**	
Pubic Hair	Coarse, curly, abundant, but amount less than mature adult	Pubic Hair	Resembles adult type, but less quantity, coarse, curly
Breasts	Areola and papilla form secondary mound	Penis	Larger, glans and breadth increase in size
		Testes	Larger, scrotum darker
Stage V		**Stage V**	
Pubic Hair	Adult feminine triangle, spread to medial surface of thighs	Pubic Hair	Adult distribution, spread to medial surface of thighs
Breasts	Mature, nipple projects, areola part of general breast contour	Penis	Adult
		Testes	Adult

Labia — folds of skin or "lips" which surround the hymen and the vaginal opening. The labia minora are the smaller, more internal folds which directly surround the hymen and vaginal opening. In young girls, these are completely hidden by the larger, more external labia majora.

Perineum — the region between the vulva and anus in a female or the scrotum and anus in the male.

Vaginal introitus — the vaginal opening, the small canal through which the penis enters during intercourse, and through which the adolescent menstruates. In children or adolescents who have not had penetration or sexual intercourse, the vaginal introitus is partially covered by the hymen, which usually has a central opening.

Vulva — the female external genitalia

Urethral orifice — the opening through which the child urinates.

The physician may need to examine the vagina for foreign bodies or bleeding by means of an *otoscope*, a small instrument commonly used to examine the ears. In older children, the physician may choose to use a small speculum, not the same size as used with adult women, or a *vaginoscope*. A more recently employed instrument used in these examinations is the *colposcope*, which provides a magnified view of the genitalia. Although this instrument was originally used to examine the cervix for the diagnosis of cancer, it is now also used as an aid in identification of genital anomalies or variations. One of the most advantageous aspects of colposcopic examination is that the instrument can be equipped with a camera that provides photographic documentation of the exam. Again, the colposcope is like a specialized light and does not touch the child. A complete exam for a prepubertal child with suspected sexual abuse does not necessarily require the use of a colposcope, and rarely requires a speculum.

Another technique which may be used for detecting small lesions of the posterior fourchette (the six o'clock region by the vaginal opening) is the use of a dye called *toluidine blue*. When the dye is swabbed onto the perianal area, small, previously unnoticed lesions appear as darker, deeply stained regions.

The absence of genital trauma does not indicate that sexual abuse has not occurred. Most people imagine sexual abuse of a child by an adult as a brutal and violent act involving forcible penetration of the vagina or rectum. This, however, is not necessarily the case. Thus, even penile penetration may not cause bruising or severe cuts which lead to permanent scarring. Additionally, rapid and significant healing can occur.

a. *Hymen*
One of the areas which the doctor will examine in the female victim is the hymen, the mucous membrane which partially covers the entrance to the

Figure 2

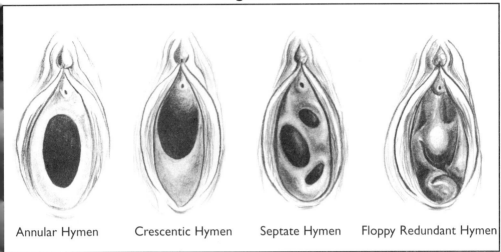

| Annular Hymen | Crescentic Hymen | Septate Hymen | Floppy Redundant Hymen |

vagina. Normal hymens can have different configurations. The most common are "annular," "crescentic," and "floppy redundant." (See Figure 2)

Other normal variations can occur although these are less common - "septate," "imperforate" (without an opening), "punctate" (with a pinpoint opening), or "cribriform" (several pinpoint openings). Studies indicate that although variations in the anatomy of the hymen occur, all newborns are born with hymens.

The physician will look for any unusual injuries or scars. The most important aspect of the exam is determining what may be a naturally occurring variation from those caused by sexually abusive or accidental trauma. In her investigation, the physician may refer to *hymenal clefts* (dips or elongated openings), or *hymenal bumps*. Although these can be indicators of abuse, both are also found in nonabused girls. If the cleft or "dips" in the hymen extend to the vaginal wall, then this indicates a transection caused by penetration through the hymen. Likewise, if the bumps are mounds of scar tissue instead of softer, fatty-like tissue, then this, too, indicates direct trauma to the hymen. An *attenuation* of the hymen refers to a small "rim" or border which represents actual decrease in the amount of hymenal tissue.

b. *Vaginal opening*

Another area which the physician will examine is the vaginal *introitus*, or opening. As with the hymen, he will look for any signs of physical trauma such as recent tears or scars. Tears occurring from attempted or completed penile penetration often occur near the six o'clock position, while those occurring from digital penetration are found more often in the upper half of the opening.

In addition to trauma, the physician will examine the size of the hymenal ring and vaginal opening. This measurement should be taken transversely, or across the opening; the measurement from back to front is often larger. The child's position and separation techniques used while obtaining the measurement should also be noted. The significance of this measurement in determining sexual abuse has been the subject of many studies. The hymenal opening can change based on the type of hymen (see Figure 2) and the age of the child. McCann and others have studied nonabused girls of different ages and report the range of hymenal opening sizes for girls of different ages and with different examination positions and techniques. It is useful for the physician to use normal data such as this in assessing whether or not a particular hymen is abnormal.

2. Male genitalia

Glans Penis — the cone shaped head of the penis which contains the urethral orifice, or the opening through which the boy urinates.

Testes — the reproductive glands located under the penis, also known as testicles. The testes are enclosed in a sac-like pouch of skin called the *scrotum*.

Redness, bruises, "hickeys," and cuts on the shaft or glans of a boy's penis may indicate forceful sucking by a perpetrator committing fellatio. Bruises or chafing may also occur from excessive handling of the penis. Boys should be tested for sexually transmitted disease. Any discharge from the urethral opening should be investigated to identify the organism causing the problem.

Figure 3

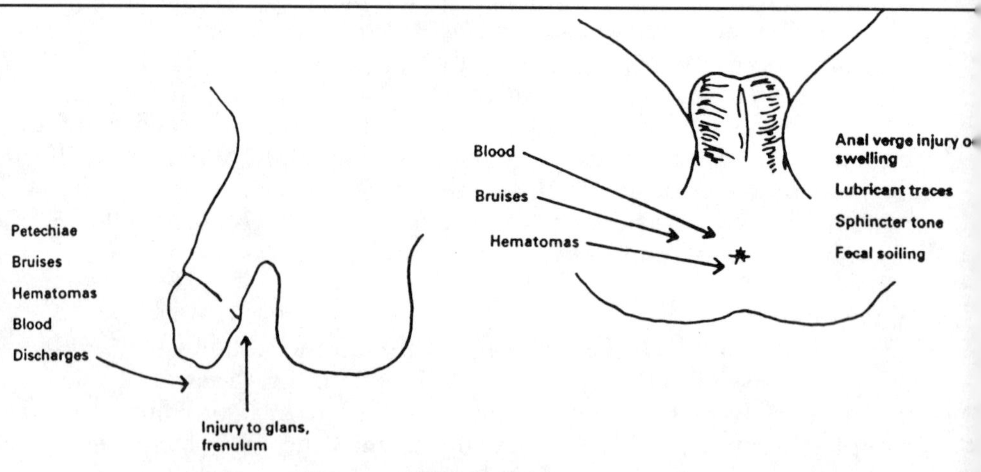

Petechiae
Bruises
Hematomas
Blood
Discharges

Injury to glans, frenulum

Blood
Bruises
Hematomas

Anal verge injury or swelling
Lubricant traces
Sphincter tone
Fecal soiling

Male Genitalia

3. *Differential for genital trauma*

In all children, genital trauma is often very painful and frightening. The thin, sensitive tissues of these organs in the prepubertal child may bleed excessively or become extremely swollen. Most parents will not hesitate to bring this type of accidental injury immediately to the emergency room, giving unsolicited, detailed explanations of the injuries. Straddle injuries resulting from horseback riding, gymnastics, or even climbing naked over the side of a tub are not uncommon. Straddle injuries result in cuts or splits in the skin and tissue over bones. Thus, the injury occurs in labia minora, labia majora, or the area around the urethra. Accidental injury to the hymen is very unusual.

Little boys may present with injuries from a scrotum that has been caught in hastily zipped trousers. In these cases, just as in all cases of suspected abuse, you should consider the developmental maturity of the child, the time elapsed before treatment, and the compatibility of the history and injury. (See "Abuse by Burns" for importance of history). Remember, children almost never purposely cause this trauma to themselves. A disclosure that a child jumped on the arm of the sofa until she was bruised and swollen is not an adequate history.

4. *Anus and rectum*

Digital or penile penetration of the anus is another frequently occurring facet of sexual abuse. Current literature suggests that boys and girls are at similar risk for this type of abuse. In a study of sexually abused boys, it was found that actual or attempted anal-penile penetration was the complaint in 62% of the victims. The degree of injury in anal penetration depends on many factors, including the size of the penetrating object, the amount of force used in the incident, the use of lubricant, and the frequency of penetration. Once the abuse has stopped, the gross physical signs of trauma can regress fairly quickly within days or weeks, even following long-lasting abuse. The doctor may refer to the anal region in the following terms.

Anus — the external opening of the large intestine.

Anal verge — the skin surrounding the anus.

Anal sphincter — the circular muscle which closes the anus.

Perianal region — the region around or close to the anus.

Rectal canal — the end portion of the large intestine that leads to the anus.

    a. *Fissures, lacerations, and hematoma*
    Depending on the size of the child, injury following penetration may vary from small cuts or bruises, to actual tears of the perianal skin,

rectal canal, or anal sphincter. Fissures or lacerations around the anus may be caused by fingernails or foreign bodies inserted into the anus. These small cuts and abrasions may leave scars which could be recognized by the physician. Penile penetration may cause anal hematomas, swellings, or masses of blood in the anal tissue. When these injuries heal they may leave anal tags, small flaps or "tags" of skin within the anus. Anal tags may also occur naturally, and may not be a sure indicator of abuse. Children who have suffered repeated episodes of anal penetration may present with thickening of the anal tissue.

b. *Anal dilatation*
Another indicator of penetration is anal dilatation, an expansion or stretching of the anus. Immediately following abuse, the anal sphincter may spasm, causing the opening to become very small and tight. This may last for up to four hours following the abuse. In cases of repeated penetration, the anal sphincter may lose its tone, or capability to close properly. In the relaxed state, the anus may appear excessively large, causing the child to unintentionally soil his or her underclothing, leading to itching, irritation, and improper hygiene. "Reflex anal dilatation", or an opening of the anus after stimulation of the surrounding skin, has been reported as a sign of sexual abuse. This is very controversial as some investigators have reported seeing this in cases of constipation.

c. *Differential for anal trauma*
• Occasionally children may suffer accidental trauma to the anus perhaps through play or from sitting on sharp objects. The history should clearly reveal this unusual form of trauma.

• Severe constipation with the passage of very large bowel movements can create fissures in the anus. Parents usually give a clear history of this problem, as well as the child, who usually experiences great discomfort.

• Children with severe diarrhea may present with swelling, redness, or chapping in the perianal area.

• As in vulvovaginal irritations, lack of proper hygiene is a frequent cause of irritation and itching in the anal region

• Occasionally children may contract a parasite known as "pinworms". These small white worms live in the upper part of the large intestine. The female creeps out of the anus and lays her eggs on the surrounding skin. These movements cause itching which the child usually scratches, causing irritation, redness, or swelling. A doctor may check for pinworms by sticking a piece of clear, transparent tape to the perineum and checking the tape under the microscope for the presence of eggs. When this problem exists, everyone living with the child should also be treated.

B. Examination following immediate abuse

If a child has been abused within the past 72 hours, he or she should be immediately examined by a physician. In addition to the examination procedures performed in any sexual abuse investigation, the physician will look for signs of recent injuries and will collect specimens to analyze for remaining sperm or a chemical called acid phosphatase, found in semen. These specimens are usually sent to a police laboratory for processing. Frequently, the examiner will look for the presence of sperm under the microscope at the time of the exam. If the child is still wearing the clothes in which she was abused, do not allow her to change or bathe. Because these may be kept for analysis and legal evidence, have her bring a change of clothing to wear home. Evidence is usually collected, clearly labeled in the presence of another witness such as a nurse or a police officer, and saved for investigation. In appropriate cases, the examiner will use a cotton-tipped swab to obtain specimens from the vagina and anus of the victim. He may also swab from the throat and gums for specimens. The doctor may pass an ultra-violet light, called a Wood's lamp, over the child's clothing and body. Substances which fluoresce a green color under this light *may* indicate seminal fluid and point out an area to swab.

1. Spermatozoa

The doctor will take specimens from the vagina, mouth, and rectum when indicated, for examination under a microscope and analysis to look for spermatozoa (sperm). The survival of spermatozoa depends on the victim's physical condition and the site of deposit. When they are deposited, most spermatozoa are *motile* (moving). Shortly after deposition, they lose the ability to move and are called *nonmotile*. When the heads separate from the tails they are termed *nonintact*. Most prosecutors regard the presence of spermatozoa as absolute proof of recent sexual contact. The fact that no spermatozoa are found does not indicate that the child was not sexually abused by penile contact because some males have little or no sperm in their ejaculate, and others may withdraw prior to ejaculation.

2. Acid phosphatase

Acid phosphatase, an enzyme present in semen regardless of the sperm count, is another laboratory test frequently performed on victims. This test can confirm if ejaculation has occurred.

3. Other tests

Other laboratory tests such as hair and fiber analysis, and ABO and DNA typing of body fluids, may also help determine the identity of the assailant. Forensic scientists continue to modify tests such as these to be more accurate.

C. Physical findings in sexual abuse

A variety of attempts have been made to classify the physical findings in sexual abuse to indicate the degree of certainty of this diagnosis. The following is adapted from Bays and Chadwick (1993) and provides a good guide for interpretation of the physical findings in the context of how concerned the physician is that sexual abuse has occurred.

1. *Specific and diagnostic findings even without a history consistent with abuse:*

   • Recovery of sperm, semen, or acid phosphatase from the body.

   • Pregnancy.

   • Fresh trauma to the genital or anal areas without a history consistent with accident.

   • Sexually transmitted diseases (specifically syphilis, gonorrhea, chlamydia, and HIV) without the history of transmission from birth or intravenous routes. Contrary to popular opinion, many sexually transmitted diseases are not acquired from inanimate objects. For example:

     Children do not acquire gonorrhea from inanimate objects such as toilet seats, bathwater, or bedsheets. Children do acquire gonorrhea from direct rubbing, mucous membrane-to-mucous membrane contact with another individual who is already infected. The bacteria that cause these infections (*Neisseria gonorrhoea*) are extremely fragile and live only within the human body. They do not survive heat, cold, or drying, and cannot live free in nature or within other animals. It is thus impossible to grow *Neisseria gonorrhoea* except under carefully controlled laboratory conditions (Sgroi, 1978).

   • Hymenal abnormalities including a markedly enlarged opening to the vagina for child's age, transections or scars, and remnants of hymenal tissue without adequate surgical or accidental history.

2. *Consistent findings: history and other supportive data may be important in diagnosis:*

   • Hymenal abnormalities with 'bumps,' notches, clefts, irregular edges, asymmetry.

   • Marked enlargement of the hymenal opening.

- Anal scars and skin tags outside the midline.

- Anal dilatation of about an inch without stool in rectal area.

- Irregularity of anal orifice with dilation.

- Specific sexually transmitted disease not acquired at birth: *Trichomonas, Condyloma acuminata, or Herpes II.*

3. **Findings often seen with sexual abuse but history and other data very important in making the diagnosis of abuse:**
- Major adhesions of the labia minora in girls out of diapers.

- Area between vaginal area and anal area (posterior fourchette) cracks and bleeds easily.

- Anal fissures.

- Thickened perianal fissures.

- A specific sexually transmitted disease which may commonly be transmitted non-sexually, e.g. bacterial vaginosis/Gardnerella vaginalis.

4. **Findings most often found without sexual abuse**
- Candida (yeast) infections.

- Redness of the hymen and surrounding areas especially in prepubertal girls.

- Hymenal variants (septate, imperforate, small bumps).

- Redness or darkening of skin around anus.

Other physical evidence of trauma that supports the child's statement (e.g., bruises elsewhere on the body if the child described being beaten; marks at the wrists and ankles if the child was allegedly tied up, etc.) should also be assessed.

In addition to the physical findings, you should look for crucial information surrounding the case from the child's family and friends. Always try to obtain corroborating statements of sexual abuse from siblings and other children in addition to adults.

V. Vaginal Irritation and Discharge in the Preadolescent Girl

The presence of vaginal discharge in the preadolescent girl usually suggests that a problem exists, possibly from infection, irritation, or a sexually transmitted disease. The physician may refer to irritation as *vulvovaginitis* or *vaginitis*, meaning inflammation of the vagina and surrounding area. The cause of the vaginitis can be by nonsexual infections or irritations, as well as by sexually transmitted infections. This section covers vulvovaginitis caused by nonsexually transmitted infection. Section VI covers sexually transmitted diseases in detail.

A. Normal vaginal discharge

Most newborn baby girls will experience a vaginal discharge, possibly with traces of blood, during the newborn period. This phenomenon is normal, and is the result of stimulation of the infant's vaginal mucosa by the mother's estrogen. It should disappear within seven to ten days. One other instance of normal preadolescent discharge occurs in the months just prior to menarche (the beginning of menstruation). Once a girl has reached adolescence, a small amount of gray-white, nonfoul-smelling discharge is normal and healthy.

B. Vaginal discharge due to nonspecific infections

1. Hygiene

Approximately 70% of cases of nonspecific vulvovaginitis (inflammation of the area around the vaginal opening) result from poor hygiene.

One of the most frequent causes of infection in children is back to front wiping, which causes fecal contamination of the vagina. In these instances, vaginal cultures may indicate particular bacteria to confirm this impression. It is important in these cases to educate both the parents and children about proper toilet training and hygiene. Repeated problems of improper hygiene may signal that the child is being improperly cared for and possibly neglected.

Another problem caused by poor hygiene is a vaginal adhesion, in which the labia minora adhere or stick together. This problem can cause pooling of urine as well as collection of feces and secretions. Such contamination results in vaginal irritation. The physician will usually treat the problem by applying an estrogen cream to the skin. Surgical cutting of the adhesions is generally only done if urine flow is being obstructed.

2. Local irritation

Other common causes of irritation and discharge are chemicals, clothing, or cosmetics. Soap products used in both bathing and laundry may cause irritation, as well as bubble bath, perfumes, and in the older adolescent, douches, and "feminine hygiene deodorants." Noncotton underwear, as well as tight-fitting jeans, panty-hose, tights, ballet leotards, rubber pants, plastic-covered paper diapers, or sanitary pads may all have a similar effect. In case of nonspecific vulvovaginitis, it is important to consider the possibility of sexual molestation with chemical irritants. For example, a case has been reported in which a four-year-old child was molested with hot peppers.

3. Foreign bodies

Foreign bodies may be the cause of vaginal irritation in a child, particularly when accompanied by a persistent, bloody, foul-smelling discharge. In these cases, the physician must inspect the vagina with a small speculum, otoscope, vaginoscope, or colposcope. The most common foreign body is rolled up wads of toilet tissue. Pubic hairs retrieved from the vagina of a prepubertal girl are an almost definite sign of abuse.

C. Specific nonsexually transmitted infections

Specific infections that are not sexually transmitted usually arise from a previously existing infection located elsewhere. Common culprits of these infections include the following:

- Parasites — one example being pinworms, the small white worms which live in the large intestine and lay their eggs on the perianal skin. Sometimes worms may actually be recovered from the vagina.

- Bacteria from the gastrointestinal tract, for example, salmonella from the child's own feces.

- Bacteria from the respiratory tract, for example, streptococcal infections from the throat of the child herself.

- Bacteria from the skin.

- Fungal infections.

VI. Sexually Transmitted Diseases (STD)

In cases of suspected sexual abuse, the physician may test the child for sexually transmitted diseases. Whether or not the physician takes cultures for STDs depends on several factors: (1) the history, (2) symptoms and physical findings, and (3) the incubation period of the specific STD organisms relative to the alleged incident. With a history of touching by hands, cultures may not be done unless there were also symptoms of abdominal or genital pain or discharge. The incubation time of a particular organism refers to the amount of time which elapses between the child's first contact with a disease and its initial appearance through cultures or various symptoms. For example, a child who has been sexually abused the day before her exam may have a negative culture for a disease which has an incubation period of 3 days. The physician may want to wait and reculture anyone who initially has a negative culture for any STD. Cultures for STDs are taken not only from the vagina, but also from the rectum and pharynx, or throat.

It is important to realize that many diseases can be transmitted both sexually and nonsexually. Mothers may pass infections to their children by (1) placental blood transfer — such as syphilis or HIV infections, or (2) passage through the birth canal. As the infant moves through the birth canal he or she receives full contact with the mother's mucous membranes, thus making the infant extra susceptible to any STD which the mother may have. Remember that it is the actual passage through the birth canal that transmits such diseases. Infants delivered through a cesarean section should not contract diseases such as genital herpes or venereal warts from the mother. In rare cases, some diseases may be transferred through fomites, meaning objects, such as toilet seats, wash-rags, or water. Some diseases may be innocently transferred from one person's hand to the vagina, anus, or mouth of another. The presence of a sexually transmitted disease in the preadolescent child is highly indicative of abuse; however, the physician must consider other modes of transmittance for some infections The following text gives a brief description of various diseases which are both sexually and nonsexually transmitted.

A. Chlamydia trachomatis

If not treated, this STD can cause pelvic inflammatory disease and/or life-long infertility. Children with this disease should also be tested for gonorrhea and trichomonas vaginalis. Doctors may test for this disease with immunologic tests or chlamydial cultures. Given a choice, the latter is currently preferred in sexual abuse cases since immunological tests have been shown to have some false positive results, particularly from the rectum. Children with positive immunological tests (or DNA probes) should be retested by culture prior to treatment.

1. *Incubation* — one to two weeks

2. *Transmittance* — can occur as the baby is born through the birth canal of an infected mother. Presence exclusively in the anal or genital areas of child indicates sexual transmittance.

B. Condyloma acuminata (venereal warts)

Condyloma acuminata causes cauliflower-like warty lesions to appear singly or in clusters in the anorectal, perineal, or genital regions as well as the larynx, pharynx, or mouth.

1. *Incubation* — six weeks to one or one and a half years.

2. *Transmittance* —can occur through vaginal births, sexual encounters, or close but nonsexual encounters from the hands to the mouth, genital or anal region of another.

It is predicted that over 50% of these cases result from sexual contact (Task Force on Pediatric Dermatology, 1984). When present in children below the age of 12, sexual abuse should be strongly suspected. These warts may be removed by burning or freezing as they may form larger tumors which have a potential risk of malignancy in the future. Smaller, fewer warts can resolve on their own without any treatment.

C. Gardnerella vaginalis

This STD is usually accompanied with a white, grey, or yellow, malodorous discharge. It does not appear frequently in prepubescent children.

1. *Incubation* — unknown.

2 *Transmittance* — can occur through sexual and nonsexual transmission. Studies suggest that it is found equally in sexually abused and normal children.

D. Genital herpes

Herpes simplex virus II is one of the most frequently diagnosed STDs in 15 to 25-year-olds. Males who carry the disease are often asymptomatic. Symptoms include the formation of very tender, painful lesions on the genitals, as well as pain in the muscles, and general discomfort (malaise). The disease may be confused with chicken pox or shingles.

1. *Incubation* — Two to 20 days, with an average of six days.

2. *Transmittance* — can occur through vaginal birth, oral-genital contact, or by the hands from the mouth to genitals. No cases have been reported of transmittance via fomites.

E. HIV (Human Immunodeficiency Virus)

Acquired Immune Deficiency Syndrome (AIDS) is a disease which breaks down the body's immune system, or its ability to fight disease. Most infected people who develop symptoms only live about two years after their symptoms are diagnosed unless aggressively treated (Centers for Disease Control), although the period of time between infection and symptoms may extend out to seven or eight years. There are many misunderstandings about the transmittance of HIV, the virus which causes AIDS.

1. *Incubation* —testing for HIV infection can only determine if a person has been exposed to the virus. Because of the time it takes for the viral antibodies to manifest themselves in the body, these tests do not always indicate their presence. In fact, a person who has been exposed may test negatively up to one year after exposure.

2. *Transmittance*—HIV can be transmitted through:

• Sexual contact in which the body secretions (such as saliva, blood, feces, semen, or vaginal secretions) of an infected person come into contact with the mucous membranes of another. This includes vaginal, anal, and oral sex.

- Shared needles of drug users, and through contaminated blood products used in blood transfusions.

- Mothers who are infected with the AIDS virus may transmit it to their infants either during pregnancy or childbirth. In fact, about one-half of pregnant mothers infected with the virus transmit it to their infants.

The virus is **not** spread through:

- Deep kissing, unless an open sore exists in the mouth.

- Sneezing or coughing.

- Touching or hugging an infected person.

- Mosquitoes.

- Fomites, such as toilet seats or door handles.

More detailed information about AIDS can be obtained by telephoning the Centers for Disease Control national hotline at (800) 447-AIDS. If you do encounter any cases involving AIDS, it is crucial that the family be referred to the proper resources in your area for up-to-date treatment and education, and counseling about the care of someone with an HIV infection.

F. Molluscum contagiosum

This virus is relatively common among both adults and children. Symptoms include the formation of pox-like sores on the skin.

1. *Incubation* — ranges from one week to six months. Therefore, contact can occur long before the lesions appear.

2. *Transmittance* — can occur either sexually or nonsexually via fomites or contact with the skin of an infected person. When determining the mode of transmittance, it is helpful to consider the site of the disease. Sores on the trunk and extremities may occur easily from play; genital sores (genital molluscum contagiosum) should arouse the suspicion of sexual abuse.

Although its presence in children and infants is usually caused by non-sexual means, the presence of molluscum contagiosum should not obviate suspicion for sexual abuse.

G. Neisseria gonorrhoea

The symptoms of this STD include discharge, swelling, painful urination, and redness, although patients may also be asymptomatic. Children who present with this disease should also be tested for syphilis, chlamydia, and trichomonas vaginalis.

1. *Incubation* — two to three days.

2. *Transmission* — can occur through vaginal birth. Primarily or always considered sexually transmitted. In a study by Drs. Branch and Paxton, 44 out of 45 one to ten-year-old girls and 115 out of 116 ten to fourteen-year-old girls contracted Neisseria gonorrhoea from documented sexual contact.

The presence of Neisseria gonorrhoea should always be considered as indicative of sexual abuse.

H. Syphilis

Syphilis occurs in the three stages. In the primary stage, the patient presents small lesions of the skin 10 to 90 days after initial contact. The secondary stage occurs two - 10 weeks after the primary stage and may cause a rash, headache, or fever. The tertiary stage occurs approximately four years later, and includes cardiovascular and neurological manifestations as well as skin, bone, and visceral lesions. Open, ulcerous lesions, or chancroids, can pass the disease when they are rubbed against another person. It is important to consider the site in which the lesions are transmitted in determining sexual abuse. The laboratory tests used in detecting these diseases are the VDRL and RPR.

1. *Incubation* — 10 to 90 days.

2. *Transmission* — sexually transmitted in more than 95% of presenting cases.

I. Trichomonas vaginalis

This STD is relatively uncommon in prepubescent children. Tests for the presence of trichomonas vaginalis include urinalysis, Pap smear, and culture. The laboratory diagnosis in males, who are commonly asymptomatic, is difficult; therefore, there is no simple way to document the perpetrator on the basis of a laboratory examination.

1. *Incubation*— days to weeks.

2. *Transmission* — can occur through vaginal birth, and rarely through fomites such as a wet washcloth. Occurs most commonly, however, through sexual contact.

Disease	Evidence of Sexual Abuse	Maternal/ Neonatal Transmission	Nonsexual Human Transmission	Transmission Via Fomites
Chlamydia trachomatis	Strong	Yes	No	No
Condyloma acuminata	Strong	Yes	Possible	No
Gardnerella vaginalis	Possible	(Studies Incomplete)		
Genital herpes	Probable	Yes	Yes for HSV-1	No
Genital molluscum contagiosum	Possible	Yes	Yes*	Yes
HIV	Strong	Yes	No**	Yes
Neisseria gonorrhoea	Strong	Yes	No	No
Syphilis	Strong	Yes	Yes***	No
Trichomonas vaginalis	Strong	Yes	No	Yes

* Transmitted through open lesions. Look at site of transmittance to determine sexual abuse.
** Transmitted through contaminated needles of intravenous drug users and blood products only. Not documented for other "fomites."
*** Transmitted through rubbing open lesions of chancroids. Look at site of transmittance to determine sexual abuse.

American Humane Association • Children's Division • Understanding the Medical Diagnosis of Child Maltreatment

VII. Treatment

A. Medical

A child who has undergone severe genital or anal trauma will usually need to sit in warm, plain water, two to three times a day. Children may be prescribed special antibiotic creams to apply to the region. The doctor may recommend that the child wear loose clothing or skirts, and clean cotton underwear. Sanitary pads should not be used at this time. Although they may seem more sanitary, they only hold in moisture and warmth, not allowing the area to "breathe."

Select antibiotics can treat most of the STDs (exceptions are condyloma, herpes, molluscum, and HIV). You need to be aware that antibiotics given for an ear infection can treat some of the STDs. It is important that cultures be obtained before treatment. The clinician may prescribe antibiotics after obtaining cultures if the likelihood is high for the child having an STD or if the cultures are positive.

It is crucial that the caretaker understand the modes of transmittance of any sexually transmitted disease which the child may have incurred through his or her abuse. Sexually active adolescents should be well educated about their disease, and the need to protect any partners. The Centers for Disease Control publish updated treatment recommendations for STDs. The local health departments, clinics, and physicians' offices will usually have current copies of these treatment guidelines.

B. Psychological

The major psychological effects of sexual abuse can be categorized into four areas: traumatic sexualization, stigma, betrayal, and powerlessness. It is important to note that each of these areas can be exacerbated by societal intervention. We recommend that children who undergo any type of sexual abuse should receive some form of counseling. Under the following cases, however, it is *essential* (Solek-Teft):

- Children who have been repeatedly abused over a long period of time by one or more offenders.

- Children who have suffered a particularly traumatic form of abuse, especially those cases in which there was a significant amount of aggression, humiliation, or embarrassment.

- Children and adolescents who have been previously abused and have subsequently become offenders.

- All cases of incest within the nuclear family.

- All cases in which there are significant short-term effects and intense symptoms such as nightmares, bed-wetting, flashbacks, phobias, or anxiety attacks.

- All cases in which the child wants to talk with an outside professional.

- Cases in which family members need advice and support in dealing with the situation.

- Cases in which there will be forthcoming legal action of a contested nature in which the child might be called upon to testify.

You should become familiar with the names of local professionals skilled in the psychological assessment of sexually abused children. If no such experts are known, refer to your local mental health agency for advice and help in these procedures.

References

American Academy of Dermatology Task Force on Pediatric Dermatology. (1984). Genital warts and sexual abuse in children. *Journal of American Academy of Dermatology, 11*, 529.

Arsenault, P., & Gerbie, A. (1986). Vulvovaginitis in the preadolescent girl. *Pediatric Annuals, 15*, 577.

Bargman, H. (1986). Genital molluscum contagiosum in children: Evidence of sexual abuse? *Canadian Medical Association Journal, 135*, 432.

Bays, J., & Chadwick, D. (1993). Diagnosis of the sexually abused child. *Child Abuse and Neglect, 17*, 91.

Branch, G., & Paxton, R. (1965). A study of gonococcal infections among infants and children. *Public Health Reports, 80*, 347.

Cantwell, H. (1987). Update on vaginal inspection as it relates to child sexual abuse in girls under thirteen. *Child Abuse and Neglect, 11*, 545.

Centers for Disease Control. (1988). Guidelines for effective school health education to prevent the spread of AIDS. *Morbidity and Mortality Weekly Report, 37*, (No. S-2).

Centers for Disease Control. (1993). Sexually transmitted diseases treatment guidelines. *Morbidity and Mortality Weekly Report, 42*, (No. RR-14).

Dattel, B., Landers, D., Coulter, K., Hinton, J., Sweet, R., & Schachter, J. (1988). Isolation of chlamydia trachomatis from sexually abused female adolescents. *Obstetrics and Gynecology, 72*, 240.

De Jong, A., & Finkel, M. (1990). Sexual abuse of children. *Current Problems in Pediatrics, 20*, 489.

Emans, S., et al. (1987). Genital findings in sexually abused, symptomatic and asymptomatic girls. *Pediatrics, 79*, 778.

Emans, S. (1992). Sexual abuse in girls: What have we learned about genital anatomy? Letter to the editor. *Journal of Pediatrics, 120*, 258.

Fuster, C., & Neinstein, L. (1987). Vaginal chlamydia trachomatis prevalence in sexually abused prepubertal girls. *Pediatrics, 79*, 235.

Gardner, J. (1992). Descriptive study of genital variation in healthy, nonabused premenarchal girls. *Journal of Pediatrics, 120*, 251.

Gardner, M., & Jones, J. (1984). Genital herpes acquired by sexual abuse of children. *The Journal of Pediatrics, 104*, 243.

Gutman, L., Herman-Giddens, M., & Phelps, W. (1993). Transmission of human genital papillomavirus disease: Comparison of data from adults and children. *Pediatrics, 91*, 31.

Hammerschlag, M., et al. (1984). Are rectogenital chlamydial infections a marker of sexual abuse in children? *Pediatric Infectious Disease, 3*, 100.

Hammerschlag, M., et al. (1985). Nonspecific vaginitis following sexual abuse in children. *Pediatrics, 75*, 1028.

Hanson, R., Glasson, M., McCrossin, I., & Rogers, M. (1989). Anogenital warts in childhood. *Child Abuse and Neglect, 13,* 225.

Hillman, D., & Solek-Teft, J. (1988). *Spiders and flies: Help for parents and teachers of sexually abused children.* Lexington, MA: Lexington Books.

Hobbs, C., & Wynne, J. (1986). Buggery in childhood — a common syndrome of child abuse. *The Lancet, 2,* 792.

Ingram, D., et al. (1986). Childhood vaginal infections: Association of chlamydia trachomatis with sexual contact. *Pediatric Infectious Disease, 5,* 226.

Ingram, D., et al. (1992). Gardnerella vaginalis infection and sexual contact in female children. *Child Abuse and Neglect, 16,* 847.

Kuhns, J. (1987). Hymens in newborn infants. *Pediatrics, 30,* 399.

McCann, J., Voris, J., & Simon, M. (1992). Genital injuries resulting from sexual abuse: A longitudinal study. *Pediatrics, 89,* 307.

McCann, J., Voris, J., Simon, M., & Wells, R. (1990). Comparison of genital examinations techniques in prepubertal girls. *Pediatrics, 85,* 182.

McCann, J., Wells, R., Simon, M., & Voris, J. (1990). Genital findings in prepubertal girls selected for nonabuse: A descriptive study. *Pediatrics, 86,* 428.

McCauley, J., Gorman, R., & Guzinski, G. (1986). Toluidine blue in the detection of perineal lacerations in pediatric and adolescent sexual abuse victims. *Pediatrics, 78,* 1039.

Muram, D., Speck, P., & Gold, S. (1991). Genital abnormalities in female friends and child victims of sexual abuse. *Child Abuse and Neglect, 15,* 105.

Neinstein, L., Goldenring, G., & Carpenter, S. (1984). Nonsexual transmission of sexually transmitted diseases: An infrequent occurrence. *Pediatrics, 74,* 67.

Schachner, L., & Hankin, D. (1985). Assessing child abuse in childhood condyloma acuminatum. *Journal of American Academy of Dermatology, 12,* 157.

Schachner, L. & Hankin, D. (1986). Is genital molluscum contagiosum a cutaneous manifestation of sexual abuse in children? Letter to the editor. *Journal of the American Academy of Dermatology, 14,* 848.

Sgroi, S. (1978). Comprehensive examination for child sexual assault: Diagnostics, therapeutic, and child protection issues. In A. Burgess, A. Groth, L. Holstrom, & S. Sgroi (Eds.), *Sexual assault of children and adolescents.* Lexington, MA: Lexington Books.

Simrel, K., Lloyd, D., Kanda, M., & Orr, L. (1988). *Medical corroborating evidence in child sexual abuse/assault cases.* Washington, DC: Children's Hospital Medical Center, Division of Child Protection.

Spencer, M., & Dunklee, P. (1986). Sexual abuse of boys. *Pediatrics, 78,* 133.

Summit, R.C. (1983). The child sexual abuse accommodation syndrome. *Child Abuse and Neglect, 7,* 177.

White, S., et al. (1983). Sexually transmitted diseases in sexually abused children. *Pediatrics, 72,* 16.

Woodling, B., & Heger, A. (1986). The use of the colposcope in the diagnosis of sexual abuse in the pediatric age group. *Child Abuse and Neglect, 10,* 111.

NEGLECT

NEGLECT

A school official calls your office with concerns of a student who might be neglected. He seems hungry and thin. He is poorly kept and looks and smells dirty. A physician voices concern about an infant who is not growing properly. Her mother seems distant, unconcerned. These and similar situations may be problems of neglect, the largest form of child maltreatment in the United States today. These cases are difficult not only in their frequency, but also in the obscurity of their diagnosis and variety of treatments. In our society, neglect is easily confused with poverty, ignorance, or parents or caretakers who are overwhelmed with other problems. The treatment of neglect is often protracted, combining the efforts of many different agencies and professionals. The physician will work with you not only in treating the child's immediate problem, but also in monitoring his growth and development through the course of his treatment. In this form of maltreatment, the combined efforts of many professionals are crucial.

In a national study of the incidence and prevalence of child abuse, the U.S. Department of Health and Human Services reports that in 1986, neglect cases outnumbered abuse cases three to two. In fact, of all cases of abuse and neglect that year, 63% involved neglect, while 43% involved abuse. The treatment of child neglect involves several different actions; many will require your exclusive interaction with a health professional. For our concerns, we have divided neglect into the categories of failure to thrive, physical neglect, medical neglect, substance abuse and neglect, safety neglect, and emotional maltreatment.

I. Failure to thrive (FTT)

Failure to thrive (FTT) is a nonspecific term applied to infants and young children who are failing to grow in a normal fashion. The diagnosis is most often made in children under the age of three years, in large part because these children are both growing quickly and dependent upon parental assistance to meet even their most basic needs. Failure to thrive may be *organic*, meaning that the growth failure is caused by an underlying disease; *nonorganic*, meaning that the cause is psychosocial in origin and not due to underlying disease; or mixed, with organic and nonorganic factors interacting.

To further complicate the matter, many children present with failure to thrive with an underlying medical condition complicated by a dysfunctional or maladaptive interaction with the parent or caretaker. It should be stated clearly that ultimately, caloric intake is the issue. Either the calories are not being offered to the child, the child is not taking the offered calories, the child is using calories at an increased rate, or the calories are not being absorbed into the body from the gastrointestinal system. Medical and psychological evaluations are needed to clarify the pattern for each child.

Maternal deprivation has been one of the traditional explanations for nonorganic failure to thrive (NOFT). It has been long known that infants deprived of touch and interaction fail to grow and die at a very high rate.

Similar patterns of growth failure have been observed in homes where the mother or caretaker may be present physically, but because of depression or other problems is unable or unwilling to provide for the infant's most basic needs.

The role of the whole family must also be considered in the assessment and, in particular, the management of children with nonorganic failure to thrive (Drotar, 1991). The family's economic and social circumstances can affect the availability of food within the household. Even if the family has an external resource, such as the Women, Infants, and Children (WIC) Supplemental Food Program available to them, dysfunction or crisis may interfere with actually obtaining the food or formula. Some families may alter the infant's diet because of well-intentioned, but erroneous beliefs about nutrition. For example, switching a two-month-old infant from breast-feeding or formula to whole milk because of concerns of "colic" or "allergies," will result in insufficient calories for growth. Additionally, in disorganized or violent families, a consistent pattern of feeding or mealtimes is either nonexistent or frequently disrupted. Thus, the infant does not receive consistent and regular caloric intake over time.

Disorders of attachment (bonding) between the parent, usually the mother, and the child typically manifest themselves after the first three months. At this time, the child needs responses and stimulation beyond simple clothing and food. While the FTT may be uncovered much later, growth failure secondary to lack of bonding can often be traced back to the second three months of life. It is important to understand that the child, by his or her nature or temperament, may be a major contributor to the parent-child interaction. Babies with colic or babies who sleep excessively and never cry, even when hungry, play a significant role in the way the parent or caretaker responds to them.

Other contributing factors to attachment disorders include marital stress, financial distress, prolonged separation between the mother and child at birth because of hospitalization, etc.

Later in the first year of life (after six months), the infant will begin to organize his or her own behaviors and develop more independence. A child who is thwarted in his endeavors may begin to "battle" his parents and assert control in those few areas open to him. Appetite is one of the few areas in which a parent cannot take control from the child. We have seen children refuse to eat when not allowed to feed themselves. Parents who insist upon maximum cleanliness during eating with constant interruptions to wipe the hands, face, plate, tray, etc., may find that the child has little interest in food.

The consequences of failure to thrive can be severe. The child, deprived of an adequate intake of calories, will break down fat and muscle to maintain growth of the brain. A child who is failing to thrive usually becomes abnormal with respect to low weight first. Subsequently, the child will slow in height growth. Small head size and delayed growth of the brain are seen as a manifestation of severe and prolonged failure to thrive. Long-term consequences, in addition to small stature, include mental retardation, behavior problems, learning difficulties, and delay in language skills.

A. When to suspect failure to thrive

Remember that the warning signals of potential failure to thrive may be apparent before the baby is ever born. If the physician is forewarned that a mother may have problems nurturing her child, he can take precautions before, during, and after the birth to help reduce these chances. Therefore, it is essential that you, as well as the physician or any clinicians involved with pregnant women, look for signals which may predict this form of neglect. A mother may need special attention if she:

- Denies the pregnancy, or fails to seek prenatal care until she is near term.

- Has attempted a self-induced abortion.

- Fails to exhibit normal "nesting" behavior in the home in preparation for the child.

- Considers putting the child up for adoption, then changes her mind at the last moment.

- Has or has had an alcohol or drug problem.

- Has or has had a psychiatric disorder, including postpartum depression.

- Has no emotional support from the baby's father, or from her family or friends.

- Has no financial support.

- Has a history of being abused or neglected herself.

- Is not able to hold, feed, or care for the child for an extended time following the birth.

Once the mother has given birth to her child, watch her behavior, or that of the caretaker, around the baby. Does she handle him roughly, like a package, or hold him close to her body? Does she talk and smile at him, or does she ignore him? Babies with nonorganic failure to thrive may present with:

- A weak, pale, and listless appearance. Instead of smiling, cooing, and maintaining eye contact, he stares vacantly with the typical "radar gaze."

- Sleeping in a bizarre, curled up, fetal position, with fists tightly closed.

- Self-stimulatory behavior, such as rocking back and forth in bed as he lays on his back (creating bald patches on the back of the head), or banging his head repeatedly against his crib.

- Dirt and feces under long, ragged fingernails, severe diaper rash, a dirty face, hands, feet, and body.

- Obvious delays in developmental and motor function. (See Appendix B, "Developmental Milestones in Infants and Children").

Although some of these cases are due to lack of money or education and can be solved with financial aid and counseling, it is still imperative that all malnourished children be examined by a physician. Not only will he or she initiate treatment for the existing malnourishment, but the doctor will also be able to monitor the child's growth and development in the future.

B. The importance of the history in FTT

One of the most important tools in determining the course of treatment for FTT is obtaining a detailed, accurate history. The physician may ask specific questions about the feeding of the infant.

- Is the child breast-fed? If so, were there any problems? If the child is not breast-fed, what formula is used? How is it prepared? How often is the child fed?

- How is the child fed? (Propping the bottle on a pillow in the crib not only suggests a lack of maternal contact, but also the possibility that the child is not getting enough food).

- How is the infant's appetite? How do you know when the child is full? (Infants who drift to sleep during feeding may be listless and apathetic from lack of stimulation, malnourishment, or may simply sleep a lot naturally).

- Has the child experienced any diarrhea or vomiting? How do the child's stools look?

In addition, the history should seek to reveal any factors other than FTT which might be the cause of the child's malnutrition.

- How large are the child's biological parents? (Genetics are often a contributing factor to a child's short stature).

- Were there any problems in the pregnancy? Was the child born prematurely? Did the mother receive adequate prenatal care?

- Is the child on any medications?

- Has the child had any serious illnesses?

• How often does the child sleep? Is the child active during waking hours?

If the doctor does not have access to the infant's mother or caretaker, your history and report to the physician should include information such as that listed above. This may require contacting previous physicians, public health nurses, or clinicians.

The physician will want to know of any factors in the psychosocial history which may indicate maternal difficulties. In addition to the "high-risk" factors listed above in section A, you should attempt, with the doctor, to determine the nature of the relationship between the mother or caretaker and the child. It is usually hard, in one conversation, to gain a true assessment of a caretaker's parenting skills or an infant's temperament. It may be helpful to ask her to describe a typical day with her infant. How often does she hold the child? Do they play together? Is the child a difficult temperament? What does she do when he cries? Many parents may purposely avoid holding or cuddling their baby for fear of spoiling the child. Others may feel that their child is rejecting them, when in reality, they simply have a less responsive child.

Once nonorganic failure to thrive is diagnosed, communication with the parents or caretakers is essential to uncover the fundamental cause of the problem and the steps to be taken to cure it. Obviously, the best time for the detection of these problems is before the infant is born. Unfortunately, many cases are not recognized until the infant is born and begins to suffer. From this pool of information, you, the physician, other counselors, clinicians, and educators can create a course of treatment and rehabilitation tailored for that family's needs. In some situations, placement outside the home may be the only solution.

C. The physician's assessment

1. Monitoring height, weight, and head circumference

In his initial assessment, the physician will obtain all previous measurements of height, weight, and head circumference and chart these on a standard growth curve. (See Figures 1 and 2) These curves can compare the infant's weight and length to those of healthy infants nationwide. This will help the physician determine if a child is small because he or she is malnourished, or small because that is the child's natural, inherited size. Obviously children's heights and weights will vary drastically according to their genetic make-up. Those whose parents are of short stature may be short themselves, with a weight in a lower percentile. If the concept of percentiles is difficult for the parent or caretaker to understand, you may want to ask the doctor for the child's age-weight. The idea that her two-year-old is the size of a one-year-old may be much more understandable to a mother than the fact that her weight is in the third percentile. In his assessment and treatment, the physician will want to monitor these measurements frequently (*See D. Treatment of FTT*). The

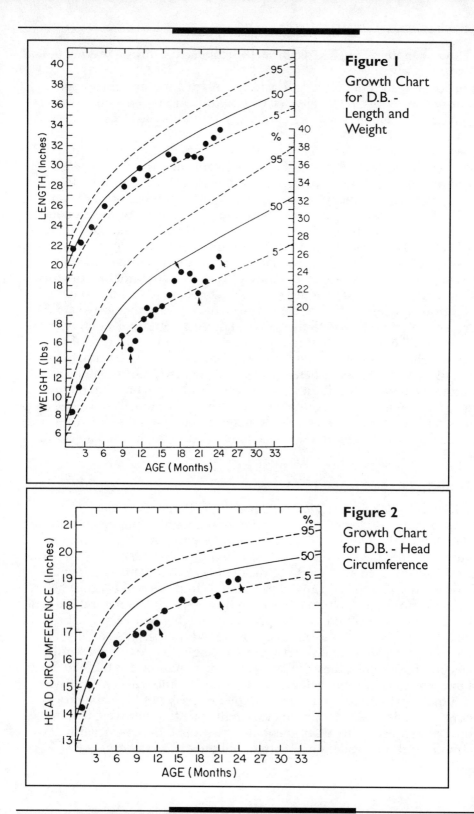

Figure 1

Growth Chart for D.B. - Length and Weight

Figure 2

Growth Chart for D.B. - Head Circumference

existence of the following conditions may arouse a doctor's suspicion of failure to thrive.

- A child whose percentile drops dramatically. For example, an infant normally existing in the 90th percentile, who drops to the 50th percentile.

- All children whose height and weight are below the 3rd percentile.

Growth charts frequently show "leveling" periods (or declines) at age periods which correspond with family stress periods. A common phenomenon in FTT children is the *"stair step"* growth which appears when the child is fed by some source other than the primary caretaker, perhaps by a visiting public health nurse, or during a stay in the hospital. Infants who undergo drastic weight gain only during these periods, with no weight gain otherwise, are classic examples of nonorganic failure to thrive. The following case history gives an example of this phenomenon.

D.B. was identified at birth as being high risk for FTT because his mother was schizophrenic. The mother was taking her medications, seeing her psychiatrist regularly, and staying with her mother and sister at home.

D.B.'s aunt accompanied him and his mother to the first two well-child visits. At about six months of age, D.B.'s mother left her mother's and stayed sometimes with D.B.'s father. She also stopped her medication and stopped seeing her psychiatrist.

D.B.'s weight went from between the 25th and 50th percentiles to the 10th at nine months of age (see arrows on Figure 1). During this time, he did not lose weight, but it was apparent from the growth chart that he was not gaining appropriately.

When ten months old, D.B. had actually lost weight, and was less than the 5th percentile - he "fell off the growth chart" for his weight. At this time, the mother was "roaming" the streets with D.B., sometimes staying with her mother or with D.B.'s father. She would forget to feed herself as well as D.B.

The clinicians contacted Child Protective Services, who helped the mother maintain residence with D.B.'s father for supervision. Two more episodes of "falling off" the weight chart occurred when D.B.'s mother left the father's home with D.B. on her own accord. Of importance, D.B.'s height and head circumference at this time (about twelve months) also began to level off. (See Figures 1 and 2)

Placement in a local residential development center showed dramatic increase in weight gain back to the 25th percentile. The father was participating in care with the goal for D.B. to be discharged to his father's home and continue to have supervised care. D.B.'s mother again assumed care in the father's home and again D.B. "fell off" the growth curve for weight, height, and head circumference. Foster care placement was initiated and D.B. again regained the 25th percentile.

2. Laboratory examination

The history and physical are the most important tools in assessing FTT. Laboratory studies can be kept to a minimum and a feeding trial in the hospital begun. The minimum studies include: a complete blood count; serum electrolytes (an analysis of sodium, potassium, bicarbonate, blood urea nitrogen, and creatinine in the blood); a urinalysis; a stool examination for blood and fat; a thyroid test; a test for cystic fibrosis; and an X-ray of the chest. If any of these preliminary studies suggest an abnormality, they should be followed up with other tests to clarify the reason for the abnormality.

3. Psychosocial evaluation

Initiating social work and dietitian interviews about feeding as soon as the medical workup has begun, instead of waiting for the medical tests to return, is very helpful. This usually involves observing a feeding with the primary caregiver and can identify problems with the interactions early in the assessment.

4. Differential

As in all abuse/neglect allegations, one of the physician's primary concerns will be to rule out any differential conditions, organic or non-organic, which may be causing the failure to gain weight. Once these are diagnosed, the child may require special treatment such as a limited diet, medications, or possibly surgery. It is important to assess the mother's /caretaker's ability to care for the child's special needs. At first, she may need help in feeding him, or taking him to and from the doctor's office. If you have concerns about the mother's capabilities in caring for a sick child, you should voice your concerns to the physician, who can help assess the situation. Problems in the following organ systems can all lead to organic failure to thrive:

- Lungs (chronic infection).

- Kidney (loss of protein or other chemicals in urine, failure of the kidney or infection).

- Intestines and stomach (chronic vomiting or poor absorption of nutrients).

- Liver (hepatitis, defect in using or processing nutrition).

- Hormone System (thyroid or adrenal gland dysfunction).

- Cardiac (heart disease with chronic failure).

It is not uncommon for new mothers/caretakers to inadvertently feed babies incorrectly, perhaps giving the wrong dilutions of formula or not feeding them enough. Other mothers may have problems breast-feeding their infant. Some babies are simply poor feeders, with poor sucking reflexes.

Although these cases are a type of nonorganic FTT, they are not necessarily volitional neglect. It is crucial that these mothers work closely with a nurse or other clinician to learn correct feeding and care of their baby.

D. Treatment of FTT

The first step in treating the FTT infant is determining his or her need for immediate hospitalization. In cases involving severe malnutrition, dehydration , or suspected physical abuse, the doctor will probably hospitalize. Sometimes, hospitalization is a routine part of assessment. Unfortunately, many nonorganic FTT children do not gain weight until the second or third week of hospitalization or longer. In fact, some actually lose weight during hospitalization, perhaps due to the various testing procedures requiring fasting, along with the actual trauma of hospitalization and separation from the home. If the infant is fed a high calorie, high protein diet and given lots of nurturing and stimulation, yet still fails to gain weight, he or she most likely has a medical problem other than nonorganic FTT.

Once nonorganic FTT is diagnosed, the goals of treatment include the following.

1. Correct the malnutrition

This is usually achieved by feeding the child a high calorie, high protein diet, with frequent feedings and a close monitoring of his or her weight, height, and head circumference. Infants may be hospitalized to achieve maximal care, or feeding can be administered out of the home, through visits by public health nurses or trips to the clinic for mother and child. Remember, it is *very* important that these infants have *constant* monitoring from day to day. In these cases you should consider:

- Does the mother have adequate transportation to the clinic? If not, has this been arranged?

- Can the mother be relied upon to keep her appointments? If not, you should consider hospitalizing the child.

- Can the mother understand, remember, and carry through with the proper feedings and nurturing of the child? If not, you should consider hospitalization.

- Can the mother afford to buy appropriate food, vitamins, medication, etc., for the child? If not, has this been taken care of?

- Does the mother have any help from family, husband, or friends? Those without support may need extra attention.

Be sure to give the doctors, nurses, and hospital social workers your name and telephone number, with the explicit request that they call you when the infant is released. You should begin your services and monitoring immediately once the mother and child have returned home.

2. *Provide nurturing and care*
Again, this must be provided either by the parents or substitutes. The parents will need support and assistance in adapting to the new styles of parenting required for the baby.

II. Physical Neglect

Children who suffer from lack of proper food, hygiene, clothing, or shelter may, in extreme circumstances, be classified as victims of physical neglect. These cases are often reported by teachers, caretakers, or neighbors, who interact with the child on a day-to-day basis.

A. Malnutrition

Malnutrition, its treatment, and its effects, are similar to those in failure to thrive babies. The differences between these two conditions is mainly the age of the child. Malnutrition is part of failure to thrive, but a child may have grown so well as an infant, that even when malnourished, he or she doesn't meet the growth failure criteria for failure to thrive. In both, it is important to remember that the neglect may not be volitional, and is often caused by poverty and lack of education. However, it is harder for a parent to make mistakes feeding older children, who, unlike infants, will tell them when they are hungry.

Children who are malnourished may be drowsy and/or pale due to *anemia*, a lack of red blood cells caused by iron deficiency. They may have extended abdomens, and a generally skinny, undernourished appearance. They may have "pinched faces," prominent ribs; wasted, "wrinkled" buttocks; and thin extremities. Some children may refuse to eat, or experience vomiting and diarrhea.

The first step in diagnosing this problem will include your thorough assessment of the home environment and the reasons for the child's lack of food. It is a good idea to contact the child's school or day care facility to inquire about his or her eating habits. How much food and what does the child bring to school? How long has the problem persisted? Are the child's siblings in the same condition? (One child who suffers while her siblings do not is most likely the victim of intentional neglect.) Does the child have bizarre eating habits, for example, eating from garbage cans or drinking from the toilet? The information from these questions will also be helpful to the doctor in his or her diagnosis and treatment.

In these particular cases, the role of the physician is similar to his or her role in the diagnosis and treatment of FTT. First, he or she must confirm the existence of malnutrition and investigate for any differential medical problems. In the exam, the physician will chart the child's height, weight, and head circumference on a growth curve. It will be important to keep track of these measurements from day to day. It may be helpful to have the school nurse keep these records. The doctor may put the child on a special high calorie and/or high protein diet. If, following treatment, the child still does not gain weight, he or she may require more testing and/or removal from the home.

B. Hygiene

Sometimes, schools or day care facilities will express concern that a child is always dirty, and smells like urine, feces, or dirty feet. Some children may be covered in insect bites or have continual infestation with lice. Infants may have severe diaper rash or "cradle cap," a condition in which flaky, crusty skin appears on the scalp, face, and head. Unfortunately, one of the most harmful aspects of bad hygiene is the ostracization the child experiences as he or she is inevitably teased by his peers.

There are no set standards for when a child is "too" dirty. Obviously, cases in which the child's health is at risk should be given strict attention, but usually, the course of action is that of education, both for the parents and the child. It is best to instruct parents/caretakers to bathe the child at least twice a week. The Department of Social Services should attempt to remain uninvolved in the cases of dirty children unless all other resources, such as voluntary agencies' services through the Department of Social Services, health clinic, and public health nurses have been depleted.

Severe conditions which do not improve after repeated attempts to offer the family help might, in some circumstances, be considered as a form of neglect. Any conditions such as severe diaper rash, lice, impetigo, scabies, or severe insect bites should be examined by a physician who can not only treat the child, but also help educate the parent/caretaker.

III. Medical Neglect

A young asthmatic boy is repetitively brought to the emergency room only when his condition is so severe that he immediately goes into intensive care. The parents of a girl with congenital cataracts refuse to consent to eye surgery which will prevent her eventual blindness. When a child with a treatable serious chronic disease or handicap has frequent hospitalizations or significant deterioration because the parents ignore medical recommendations, court-enforced supervision or even foster placement may be required. Some parents may refuse treatment based on religious grounds. Others are simply anxious and afraid about a disease and treatment which they do not understand.

In such circumstances, the primary goal is identifying and nullifying the parents' specific concerns about treatments or hospitalization. Although the physician will be the most knowledgeable source of information, the parents may relate more comfortably with you; as a liaison between the parents and the physician, you may play the most important role in this process. For good results, both you and the physician should attempt to include both parents in the decision process. When a physician feels that a child's need for treatment is severe enough to justify a court order, you will need to work with him or her in this endeavor.

Barton Schmitt breaks this form of neglect into clear categories which include serious acute illnesses, life-threatening chronic diseases, disabling diseases, and handicapping chronic diseases. You may experience all of these in your work, and although each case invariably differs from another, you should be familiar with these problems.

A. Serious acute illness

These are the cases usually considered emergencies. Examples are parents who refuse to allow a blood transfusion to save a child in shock, or parents who refuse to admit a severely dehydrated child to the hospital. When parents consistently refuse to sign a consent form in these circumstances, the court must intervene, and do so quickly. Also, diseases that endanger the public safety can evoke a court order if the parents refuse treatment.

B. Life-threatening chronic diseases

Chronic diseases are long-lasting ones, such as asthma or diabetes mellitus. Sometimes children with diseases such as these experience frequent medical problems because their parents/caretakers ignore medical recommendations for home treatment.

Chronic illnesses are added stresses for families, but about two-thirds of these families will cope with such stress either very well or adequately. The remaining one-third who cannot adapt adequate coping strategies to care for their chronically ill child will need identification and support to assure their child receives appropriate care.

C. Disabling or handicapping chronic diseases

These cases involve children who will develop permanent disfigurement or disability if they do not receive treatment. Examples are children with congenital glaucoma or cataracts, which will eventually develop into blindness if surgery is not performed. Although parents eventually can be persuaded of the need for surgery in these conditions, those who persist in their refusal will eventually need to be taken to courts, which can usually be swayed to intervene once the risks and benefits of treatment are reviewed.

IV. Substance Abuse and Neglect

Parental addiction to alcohol, cocaine, heroin, and other drugs has led to one of the more complex and devastating problems in child neglect and abuse. Recent studies have identified parental substance abuse as occurring in 40 to 60% of the cases of child maltreatment. The alarming rate of substance abuse occurring during pregnancy has been well documented during the last decade, with estimated illegal drug use identified in 10 to 24% of all pregnancies. The problem of parental addiction thus encompasses all aspects of child maltreatment - physical abuse; sexual abuse; physical, emotional, and medical neglect; and additionally, the potential of harm to the infant during the prenatal period.

A. Pregnancy and substance abuse

Pregnant women who are addicted to drugs or alcohol are at far greater risk for a range of medical problems which adversely affect the health of the mother and the developing fetus. Drug-dependent mothers have an increase in obstetrical problems such as poor nutrition, anemia, and infections including tuberculosis. Often prostitution is used to provide money to support their habit thus creating an even greater risk to contract sexually transmitted diseases, and HIV infection in particular, leading to serious problems for both the mother and unborn child. Cocaine use, which causes constriction of blood vessels, has been documented to lead to a variety of major obstetrical complications such as infections of the amniotic fluid and sac, premature rupture of the membranes (which protects the fetus from infections), abruptio placenta (an early separation of the placenta leading to loss of blood and oxygen supply to the fetus), intrauterine growth retardation, and premature birth.

The pregnant, addicted woman is less likely to seek or adequately follow through on routine prenatal care although their pregnancies are usually high-risk and could benefit most from even closer care than other pregnancies. In addition to the direct risks to their own health such as infections, high blood pressure, malnutrition, and bleeding; pregnant, addicted women are more likely to be physically abused themselves. All of these complications can lead to a high rate of spontaneous abortions and, for those infants who reach delivery, serious problems. Mothers who do not receive prenatal care are more likely to give birth to low birth weight infants and these babies are more likely than a normal birth weight infant to die during the first four weeks of life.

Because these infants are born prematurely, have low birth weights, and acquire infections at birth and prenatally from the mother, they are at increased risk for all the problems related to these conditions, such as requiring mechanical ventilation and oxygen to breathe, bleeding into the brain from rupture of small fragile blood vessels, overwhelming infections needing antibiotics, and an inability to suck effectively, leading to artificial feeding. Infants exposed prenatally to cocaine, heroin, and methadone can experience life threatening withdrawal symptoms shortly after birth so that physicians now are constantly on the lookout for problems in the delivery room unique to the resuscitation of such a baby. In the immediate newborn period, infants exposed to cocaine exhibit problems with irritability making these babies difficult to console.

When pregnant mothers drink, the alcohol can cause problems described as Fetal Alcohol Syndrome (FAS). The unique infant traits associated with fetal alcohol syndrome include the following:

• An unusual face, including droopy eyelids and smaller than usual eye slits.

• Active alcohol withdrawal symptoms after birth.

• Congenital heart defects.

- Low birth weight and sustained smallness in size for age.

- Moderate mental retardation.

The negative impact of drugs and alcohol on the development of infants is well documented when problems such as those discussed above exist. Sudden Infant Death Syndrome (SIDS) is reported to be higher in cocaine exposed babies, but other studies contradict this. Some infants can become "boarder babies" and are essentially abandoned, or their mothers have died from an AIDS-related infection or obstetrical complications associated with substance abuse.

There is still much controversy in the studies of long-term impact of prenatal exposure to substances such as cocaine, if the infant is lucky enough not to have immediate problems. Most current research points to the powerful impact of the environment of substance abusing caregivers on the development of the child making it difficult, if not impossible, to separate prenatal effects from those caused postnatally.

Prenatal screening for substance abuse can be useful to identify high-risk pregnancies and offer close care and support to the pregnant mother. Unfortunately, a major obstacle to obtaining prenatal care is the lack of programs designed specifically for addicted pregnant mothers. Most drug treatment programs have focused on males and not on the unique issues of women and their special needs during pregnancy. Another obstacle to obtaining prenatal care is the fear of retribution and the all too frequent desire to punish the pregnant woman.

Comprehensive programs that can identify the addicted mother, offer drug addiction treatment, and provide necessary support services are most likely to meet the unique needs of substance abusing mothers. These services would include adequate housing, counseling for sexual and domestic violence, child care, health care (including family planning and well-child care, in addition to prenatal care), education, training, and employment.

B. The family and substance abuse

The combined stresses of substance dependency and demands of infants and children for routine care can create a volatile environment in which physical neglect or abuse are very likely to occur. One study of parental substance abuse and child maltreatment showed alcohol abuse to be significantly related to physical abuse but not sexual abuse, while cocaine abuse was the opposite, with a significant association to sexual abuse but not physical abuse. Severe neglect can occur by the actual physical absence of the parent because of drug-seeking behaviors, prostitution, or actual incarceration. Drug addiction and participation in drug trafficking create, in both the child and family's social environment, a volatile climate with frequent exposures to actual violence. Even if the parents themselves are not drug abusers, the witnessing of violence can impact child development by the direct observation of shootings, knifings, etc., and changes in caregiving practices such as restricting the child's outdoor activities.

Parents who are high on drugs or alcohol cannot provide the very basic needs of infants and children for food, hygiene, and sleep, let alone respond to the more subtle cues for physical and social interactive nurturing. Some addicted parents may also have concurrent personality disorders magnifying the distortions of parent-child interactions.

Addicted parents have impaired judgement and can consciously or unconsciously "use" their children to help deal with their addiction problem. This can be as obvious as prostituting a child for money to buy drugs, to the more subtle plan of a mother to breast-feed her baby with the mistaken assumption it will help her "stay clean."

Most substance abusing families have a multitude of other problems that create an environment of high risk for child maltreatment. Current research would indicate that continued parental addiction easily can prevent or undo other interventions. Thus, there is a real need to provide effective treatment programs for addicted parents and provide protection for children whose parents refuse or fail at these treatment efforts.

V. Safety Neglect/Environment injurious to the welfare of the child

Barton Schmitt defines safety neglect as any situation where an injury occurs because of gross lack of supervision. This might involve leaving poisons, open heaters, knives, or guns within the child's reach. Repeated dog bites by the family dog also represents a dangerous home environment. Obviously, every child will sustain minor injuries or traumas during the childhood years. No parent can watch an infant or young child every minute of the day. It is when these accidents are repeated and severe that physicians and social workers should become concerned with neglect. It is estimated that before the age of three, children have not developed an adequate sense of safety awareness; normally, children below this age should not be allowed the freedom and independence that lead to serious injuries.

Parents will need education on child safety; they may need financial help in making their home "accident proof;" for example, placing screens around open heaters, putting plugs in electrical outlets, using smoke detectors, or placing safety catches on cabinets. One indicator of safety neglect is the parents' or caretakers' concern for the child. Watch how they handle the child and react to his injury. If a baby who has fallen off the sofa is brought to the doctor and then left unattended on the examining table, one should be concerned about the parent's ability or desire to protect that child.

Ideally, if a physician reports an injury which he or she considers a product of gross safety neglect, you would investigate any hospitals, doctors, or clinics which might have records of previous accidents. If the child is new to your agency, you might need to look out of the county or even to another state for this information. This time-consuming and often frustrating process may seem meaningless at times, but may uncover critical problems which need to be treated. In your history, ask the parents/caretakers questions about specific injuries which might have occurred; for example:

- Has the child had any previous fractures or broken bones? If so, what were the circumstances surrounding each event?

- Has the child ever accidentally ingested poisonous substances? If so, what was the substance and where was it located in the home? What precautions have you taken to avoid this problem in the future?

- Has the child had any previous burns? How severe were they? How exactly did they happen?

- What other accidents has the child had and how serious were they?

VI. Emotional Maltreatment

This section will expose you briefly to some definitions, high-risk factors, results, and assessment styles for emotional maltreatment. Our discussion will pertain to emotional maltreatment considered both neglectful and abusive. The Psychologically Battered Child , by James Garbarino, Edna Guttmann, and Janis Wilson Seeley, provides an excellent comprehensive discussion of emotional abuse and neglect. Much of the text in this section was adapted from this book.

A. Definition

In North Carolina, emotional maltreatment refers to:

Any juvenile below 18 years of age whose parents or other caretakers create or allow to be created serious emotional damage to the juvenile and refuse to permit, provide, or participate in its treatment. (N.C. General Statute 57A-507 (1) (d), 1983)

Unfortunately, this definition is purposely vague in most courts across the nation. Instead of actually *defining* emotional maltreatment, most laws simply *refer* to it, leaving the exact legal interpretations to the individual courts. Emotional maltreatment is far more prevalent than most people think; an estimated 3.4 children per 1,000 suffer each year in the United States (U.S. Department of Health and Human Services, 1988). Garbarino, Guttmann, and Wilson Seeley divide emotional maltreatment into five categories: *rejecting, terrorizing, ignoring, isolating,* and *corrupting.* The following explanations of these divisions were adapted from their text.

1. Rejection
Rejection involves those behaviors which constitute abandonment. "Mild" rejection is confined to isolated incidents, while "moderate" and "severe" are more frequent and more generalized. During infancy this may involve abandonment or refusing to return smiles and vocalization. For older children, it might involve leaving the child home from family outings, belittling or scapegoating the child, or subjecting the child to verbal humiliation and criticism.

2. Terrorizing

Parents/caretakers who terrorize their children intentionally stimulate intense fear by threatening them with extreme or sinister punishment, thus creating an environment of unpredictable threat. During infancy this may involve teasing and scaring the child, or reacting with extreme responses to infantile behavior. For older children, it may involve intense direct threats to the child's everyday sense of security.

3. Ignoring

Ignoring refers to parents/caretakers who are so psychologically preoccupied with themselves and their surroundings that they are unable to respond to the child's psychological needs. These parents/caretakers may erect a "barrier of silence" in the child's presence, and refuse to engage in conversation or show interest in his or her daily activities, concentrating on other relationships which displace the child as an object of affection.

4. Isolating

Isolating involves those behaviors that rob the child of his or her opportunity to develop normal social relations. These parents/caretakers teach their children to avoid social contact beyond the parent-child relationship, punishing them for making social overtures to other children or adults.

5. Corrupting

"In general, corrupting refers to parental behaviors that 'mis-socialize' children and reinforce them in antisocial or deviant patterns, particularly in the areas of aggression, sexuality, or substance abuse. Such behaviors tend to make the child unfit for normal social experience" (Garbarino, Guttmann, Wilson Seeley, 1986).

B. "High-risk" factors in emotional abuse

As in all forms of neglect and abuse, there are certain conditions which signal families who are at "high-risk" for emotional maltreatment. The following is a summation from the current literature on the subject.

1. Environment:
- Families are socially isolated.

- Poverty, unemployment, and/or poor housing conditions.

- High crime.

- Services from outside sources unavailable.

- Large families.

2. *Parents:*

• Depressed.

• Alcohol or substance abuse problems.

• In a state of bad health.

• Lack knowledge of child development.

• Disagreement of parenting skills between parents.

• Sanction severe corporal punishment.

• Marital problems.

• Low self-esteem.

• Abused or neglected themselves.

3. *Child:*

• Has behavior problems in the home.

• Has special handicaps.

• Is emotionally disturbed.

C. Results of emotional maltreatment

It is impossible to construct a list of "symptoms" of emotional maltreatment. Individual children are all unique in their sensitivity and vulnerability to this form of maltreatment. While some children will manifest clear psychological and/or physical delays, others may not react at all. Listed below are some of the various emotional and physical responses to emotional maltreatment.

Emotionally, the child has a very low sense of self-esteem. He or she may show withdrawn, apathetic behavior, or react with aggression and hostility. The child is often paranoid, distrustful, and fearful of others. Because so much attention is centered on the caretaker and his or her emotional needs, the child learns to ignore his or her own feelings. Often, the child cannot interact with other people because he or she has never learned how to do so. As the child matures into an adult, these problems persist. He or she has an increased sensitivity to crises, with a decreased ability to cope with normal problems.

Physically, the signs of emotional neglect are similar to those of failure to thrive. The child may experience delays in motor ability and development of language. As in other forms of neglect, his or her physical growth may be affected.

It is important to remember that children may react in these ways to any stresses in their environment. Examples may include divorce, death of a close relative, births, stepparents, unemployment of a caretaker, or a change of residence. Assessing emotional maltreatment involves the parent/caretaker just as much as it does the child, for it is only when the parent's behavior as well as the child's reaction prove insufficient that abuse can be determined.

D. Assessment

The assessment of emotional abuse is mainly a psychological one, which, for our purposes, is not covered in this manual. It is our recommendation that you involve the entire family in psychological counseling and utilize the advice of experienced professionals in that field in making decisions in these cases.

REFERENCES

Bays, J. (1992). The Care of Alcohol- and Drug-Affected Infants. *Pediatric Annals, 21,* 485.

Baucher, H., et al. (1988). Risk of sudden infant death syndrome among infants with in utero exposure to cocaine. *Journal of Pediatrics, 113,* 831.

Cantwell, H. (1978). S*tandards of neglect.* Denver, CO: Denver Department of Social Services.

Drotar, D. (1991). The family context of nonorganic failure to thrive. *American Journal of Orthopsychiatry, 16,* 23.

Egeland, G., & Vaughn, B. (1981). Failure of "bond formation" as a cause of abuse, neglect, and maltreatment. *American Journal of Orthopsychiatry, 5,* 78.

Evans, D., et al. (1980). Intellectual development and nutrition. *Journal of Pediatrics, 97,* 358.

Famularo, R., Kinscherff, R., Bunshaft, D., Spivak, G., & Fenton, T. (1989). Parental compliance to court-ordered treatment interventions in cases of child maltreatment. *Child Abuse and Neglect, 13,* 507.

Famularo, R., Kinscherff, R., & Fenton, T. (1992). Parental substance abuse and the nature of child maltreatment. *Child Abuse and Neglect, 16,* 475.

Famularo, R., Stone, K., Barnum, R., & Wharton, R. (1986). Alcoholism and severe child maltreatment. A*merican Journal of Orthopsychiatry, 56,* 481.

Garbarino, J., Guttmann, E., & Wilson Seeley, J. (1986). *The psychologically battered child.* San Francisco:Jossey-Bass Publishers.

Horan, P.A., Gwynn, C., & Renzi, D. (1986). Insulin-dependent diabetes mellitus and child abuse: Is there a relationship? *Diabetes Care, 9,* 302.

Jaudes, P.K., & Diamond, L.J. (1986). Neglect of chronically ill children. *American Journal of Diseases in Childhood, 140,* 655.

Kempe, R.S., & Goldbloom, R. (1980). Malnutrition and growth retardation ("failure to thrive") in the context of child abuse and neglect. In C.H. Kempe & R.E. Helfer (Eds.), *The battered child.* Chicago, IL:The University of Chicago Press.

Murphy, J.M., et al. (1991). Substance abuse and serious child mistreatment: Prevalence, risk, and outcome in a court sample. *Child Abuse and Neglect, 15,* 197.

Oates, R.K., Peacock, A., & Forrest, D. (1984). Development in children following abuse and nonorganic failure to thrive. *American Journal of Diseases in Childhood, 138,* 764.

Rosenn, D., Stein, L., & Bates, M. (1980). Differentiation of organic from nonorganic failure to thrive syndrome in infancy. *Pediatrics, 66,* 698.

Schmitt, B., & Kempe, C.H. (1975). The pediatrician's role in child abuse and neglect. *Current Problems in Pediatrics, 5,* 3.

Taylor, L., Zuckerman, B., Harik, V., & Groves, B. (1994). Witnessing violence by young children and their mothers. *Journal of Developmental and Behavioral Pediatrics, 15,* 120.

U.S. Department of Health and Human Services. (1988). *Study findings: Study of national incidence and prevalence of child abuse and neglect.* Washington, DC: National Center on Child Abuse and Neglect, U.S. Department of Health and Human Services.

Wasserman, D.R., & Leventhal, J.M. (1993). Maltreatment of children born to cocaine-dependent mothers. *American Journal of Diseases in Childhood, 147,* 1324.

APPENDIX A
WELL-CHILD CARE AND IMMUNIZATIONS

All infants and children need immunizations against the preventable childhood diseases as a cornerstone of their health care. Many of these immunizations are required before children can enter school. All immunizations, both required and recommended, should be given at the appropriate ages to prevent death and disability from these serious infections.

The American Academy of Pediatrics provides recommendations for immunizations and minimal standards for well-child check-ups, which coincide with the immunization schedule. The child's development and physical growth are assessed at these regular visits.

1. Minimal standards for well-child check-ups

> a. One visit before 2 months.
> b. One visit between 2 and 6 months.
> c. One visit between 6 and 12 months.
> d. One visit between 12 and 18 months.
> e. One visit between 18 and 24 months.

2. Immunization

Although children are not allowed to enter school unless they have been immunized, this important part of well child-care should be started long before the child enters school, as early as the first days of life. Unfortunately, some parents/caretakers are ignorant about the immunization process. They may delay taking the child to clinic, thinking they can "catch-up" later, and give them all at one time. If parents/caretakers do not understand this process, it needs to be explained to them by a health care provider, who, in turn, should keep adequate records of the baby's shots. Because the shots are free at any public health clinic or federally funded immunization program, financial problems should not interfere with this process. If a child has not received any shots by the first one and a half years of age, the county health department should intervene and help the family with this problem. Those who have not received shots will require a special "catch-up" schedule, which is listed in the American Academy's *1994 Red Book Report of the Committee on Infectious Diseases*, generally available in Public Health Departments, health clinics, and medical providers' offices. Whoever is helping the family with the "catch-up" should ask for a copy of the whole schedule to make sure the child returns at the right times to complete the series.

Recommended Schedule for Active Immunization of Normal Infants and Children

Age	Immunization
birth	HBV
2 months	DTP*, OPV*, HBV, Hib
4 months	DTP*, OPV*, Hib
6 months	DTP*
12-15 months	MMR*, Hib
15-18 months	DTP*, OPV*, HBV
4-6 years	DTP*, OPV*, MMR*
14-16 years	Td* every 10 years throughout life

*Required immunizations for school admissions

Explanation of diseases represented by abbreviations

DTP	Diptheria, Tetanus, Pertussis (whooping cough)
HBV	Hepatitis B virus Vaccine
Hib	Haemophilus influenza type b
OPV	Oral Poliovirus Vaccine
MMR	Measles, Mumps, Rubella
Td	Tetanus (adult dose), diptheria

APPENDIX B
DEVELOPMENTAL MILESTONES IN INFANTS AND CHILDREN

In the course of an infant's development, the physician will monitor the stages of his or her physical and neurological growth. Of course, each child will differ in his own particular course of growth, but the patterns of normal development are relatively consistent. If you are working with a parent whose child's development seems inconsistent or abnormal, you should advise him or her of the appropriate resources to have the child examined.

An important factor in a child's development is his or her temperament, which will be unique for each child. Assessments of temperament include assessing the child's activity level, the rhythmicity of his or her biologic functions such as sleep-wake cycles and the regularity of hunger and elimination, the child's reactions to new situations, his or her adaptability over time to new situations, the level of intensity of a stimulus necessary to set off a reaction, the intensity of his responses to stimulus, his distractibility, and his attention span and persistence.

Research has shown that most children have similar clusters of characteristics which produce recognizable temperament styles, all of which are "normal." About 10% of the children in one study displayed a "difficult child" syndrome, characterized by having "irregular biologic functions, intense withdrawal responses to new situations, slow adaptability over time, and a predominantly negative mood" (Chamberlain, 1980). Babies who display characteristics such as these are at higher risk of being abused. Likewise, their parents or caretakers may become frustrated, and are likely to feel that they are doing something radically wrong. They will need extra support in terms of reassurance from the physician and social worker. Another 10% of the children in the study displayed "slow to warm up" characteristics. These children have similar characteristics to the "difficult child," however, their reactions are ones of quiet withdrawal rather than active protests. These "quiet" children may be at a higher risk of being neglected inadvertently because they do not cry to give parents signals when they are hungry or in pain. Fortunately, most children in this study displayed a cluster of characteristics that produced an "easy child" with regular biologic rhythms, a positive approach to new situations, and a predominantly positive mood (Chamberlin, 1980).

In your general assessment of a case, you should keep these characteristics in mind. Through your brief interaction with the child, try to gain a clearer picture of which of these normal categories he or she fits into. Ask the mother or caretaker questions about her interactions with the child which may reveal the child's temperament. In his or her physical examination, the physician will also try to assess the child for these characteristics.

Following is a list of developmental milestones which physicians look for in their well-child check-ups. Remember, no child will follow these stages exactly. Tests for monitoring a child's developmental growth are available and the forms are often included in clinic charts similar to those for growth. Dr. Frankenburg and colleagues have constructed two widely used developmental tests - the Revised Prescreening Developmental Questionnaire (R-PDQ) and the Denver Developmental Screening Test-Revised (DDST-R). You can ask the family or the health care provider how the child is maturing relative to standardized screening tests such as these.

A. Gross Motor

2 mos	- head control
4 mos	- rolls, no head lag
6 mos	- sits, crawls
9 mos	- pulls to stand
12 mos	- walks
15 mos	- walks up stairs, walks backwards
18 mos	- kicks, throws
24 mos	- jumps, pedals, stands on one foot
30 mos	- broad jumps
36 mos	- stairs alternating, stands on one foot for 5 seconds
4-6 yrs	- skips, catches ball

B. Fine Motor

2 mos	- hand to mouth
4 mos	- grasps, reaches, hand to midline
6 mos	- transfers, drops, unilateral reach
9 mos	- radialized rake
12 mos	- pincer grasp
15 mos	- scribbles
18 mos	- stacks 4 cubes
24 mos	- stacks 8 cubes
30 mos	- draws a horizontal line
36 mos	- copies circle, imitates bridge
4-6 yrs	- copies square, draws a person

C. Language

2 mos	- social smile, reciprocal vocalizations, laughs
4 mos	- coos, imitates, turns to voice
6 mos	- babbling
9 mos	- Mama/Dada (nonspecific)
12 mos	- Mama/Dada (specific)
15 mos	- 3-6 words, jargon
18 mos	- combines 2 words
24 mos	- combines 3 words, plurals, 2 stage command
30 mos	- pronouns, prepositions
36 mos	- compound sentences, 3 stage commands
4-6 yrs	- mature usage, articulation

D. Social

4 mos	- caregiver preference, sleep cycles
6 mos	- stranger wariness
9 mos	- autonomy (self feed)
12 mos	- autonomy ("No"); sexual identification
15 mos	- removes clothes, temper tantrums
18 mos	- renewed separation problems
24 mos	- ability beyond judgement, temper, negativism
30 mos	- interactive games
36 mos	- identifies gender differences, empathy
4-6 yrs	- mastery, fantasy

E. Cognitive

2 mos	- visual tracking
4 mos	- watches hands, follows dropped object
6 mos	- knows individuals
9 mos	- object permanence
12 mos	- appropriate use of objects
15 mos	- identifies use of objects
18 mos	- identifies indirect causes
24 mos	- identifies hidden causes, barriers
30 mos	- pretending, knows own name
36 mos	- concept of cold, hungry, tired, one color
4-6yrs	- explanations, stories, defines words

REFERENCES

Chamberlin, R. (1980). Behavioral problems and their prevention. *Pediatrics in Review,* 2: 14.

Frankenburg, W.K., Ker, C.Y., Engelke, S., et al. (1988). Validation of key Denver Developmental Screening Test items: A preliminary study. *Journal of Pediatrics,* 112: 560.

Frankenburg, W.K., & Thornton, S.M. (1987). Revision of the Denver Prescreening Developmental Questionnaire. *Journal of Pediatrics, 110*: 653.

APPENDIX C
CHILD ABUSE FATALITIES
THE ROLE OF THE MEDICAL EXAMINER

When a person dies suddenly and unexpectedly or as a result of trauma in North Carolina, the county Medical Examiner assumes jurisdiction of the body to determine cause and manner of death. Cause of death is the disease or injury that was responsible for the death. *Manner of death* is an explanation of how the cause arose and can be natural (nontraumatic, medical causes) or unnatural (homicide, suicide, or accident). Deaths may also be certified as undetermined as to cause and manner if the Medical Examiner is unable to ascertain how and from what the person died. In order to make a determination of cause and manner of death, a Medical Examiner may order an autopsy as part of the medico-legal investigation of death. Whether or not an autopsy is performed, all Medical Examiner cases undergo investigation and a report is filed at the Office of the Chief Medical Examiner. These reports, as well as autopsy reports, are public records.

Child abuse fatalities are classified as homicides. Before this determination is made, the Medical Examiner must gather information from the professionals who were involved in the criminal investigation, most often the police, as well as medical and social information which the social services worker may be in a position to provide. The Medical Examiner has legal access to all records that may assist him or her in determining cause and manner of death.

The investigation of child abuse fatalities requires careful consideration of scene or environmental information. The exact physical circumstances of how a child was injured may provide critical clues to identify a case of possible abuse. Who gathers that information is not as critical as that it be taken into account. Emergency Medical Services, Law Enforcement, and other first responders are often in the best position to obtain this data.

The Medical Examiner's report of investigation is a separate document from the autopsy and contains identifying information, cause and manner of death, and a chart which shows any external injuries present. A narrative is included which often contains important historical facts.

Homicides and any suspicious deaths should always have a complete autopsy performed. In the case of child abuse fatalities, this is usually done by a trained forensic pathologist who has expertise in the medical detections of child abuse, and may not be the Medical Examiner who assumed jurisdiction of the body. Components of the autopsy report include:

A. *Pathologic diagnosis* — This is a summary of abnormal findings and may include diagnoses that are unrelated to the cause of death. The traumatic injuries that are responsible for a child abuse death should be listed first.

B. *Cause of death* — The disease or injury that was responsible for the death will be stated succinctly.

C. *External description* — This includes identifying information such as height, weight, hair color, clothing, and evidence of medical intervention (resuscitation) if present.

D. *Evidence of injury* — Any bruises, abrasions, or other injuries that are found on the body are described in detail here.

E. *Additional procedures* — In child abuse cases, the pathologist may order X-rays looking for unsuspected healing or acute fractures. Cultures may be taken for suspected infectious processes. Special evidence collected, such as body hairs or samples for semen analysis, will be documented. In addition to alcohol levels, which are performed on all Medical Examiner cases, special chemistry tests may be done looking for other drugs.

F. *Internal Examination* — In this section, the pathologist lists by organ system the positive and negative physical findings. Often it is helpful to look at "musculo-skeletal system" for evidence of rib fractures. Many times any positive findings will be referred to as "see description of injury" or other relevant section.

G. *Microscopic Examination* — The pathologist routinely takes samples of major organs to examine under the microscope. Sometimes unsuspected inflammation may reveal a natural cause of death, or microscopic examination of a fracture may help the pathologist ascertain its age.

H. *Neuropathologic Consultation* — Because an infant's brain is soft and difficult to cut, the pathologist may opt to fix the brain in formalin for several days to two weeks and then examine it for evidence of injury or disease. This is often done in suspected child abuse cases where head trauma may lead to the lethal injury. The eyes may also be examined for the presence or absence of retinal hemorrhages which may support the diagnosis of shaken-impact syndrome.

I. *Summary and Interpretation* — In these few paragraphs, the pathologist will give known and pertinent history and any significant autopsy findings. This will lead into and support the pathologist's opinion as to the cause of death.

J. *Toxicological Findings* — This details the results of any studies for alcohol or other drugs or toxins in samples taken at autopsy. Cases are routinely screened for alcohol. Other drugs ordinarily are looked for only when something in the history indicates the likelihood of their presence.

This is the suggested format for a medico-legal autopsy in North Carolina. Not all reports will be exactly the same. Many will also contain body diagrams that illustrate the location of any injuries and other external features of the body.

A completed autopsy report may take several weeks to complete. Any additional information the Child Protective Services worker can provide during the investigation may be very important to the determination of manner and cause of death. Likewise, the pathologist and Medical Examiner can provide useful information to the social worker charged with the protection of surviving siblings. Coordination between Child Protective Services, Law Enforcement, and the Medical Examiner is necessary to ensure optimal case management.

REFERENCES

Bass, M.B., Kravath, R.E., & Glass, L. (1986). Death-scene investigation in sudden infant death. *The New England Journal of Medicine, 315*, 100.

Bays, J., & Lewman, L.V. (1992). Toluidine blue in the detection at autopsy of perineal and anal lacerations in victims of sexual abuse. *Archives of Pathology and Laboratory Medicine, 116*, 620.

Helpern, M. (1976). Fatalities from child abuse and neglect: Responsibility of the medical examiner and coroner. *Pediatric Annals, 5*, 157.

Perrot, L.J., & Nawojczyk, S. (1988). Nonnatural death masquerading as SIDS. *The American Journal of Forensic Medicine and Pathology, 9*, 105.

Wecht, C.H., & Larkin, G.M. (1988). The Battered Child Syndrome - a forensic pathologist's viewpoint. *Medical Trial Quarterly, 28*, 1.

Zumwalt, R.E. and Hirsch, C.S. (1988). Pathology of fatal child abuse and neglect. In C.H. Kempe & R.E. Helfer (Eds.), *The battered child*. Chicago, The University of Chicago Press.

APPENDIX D
GROWTH CHARTS

BOYS: BIRTH TO 36 MONTHS
PHYSICAL GROWTH
NCHS PERCENTILES* Name_____ Record #_____

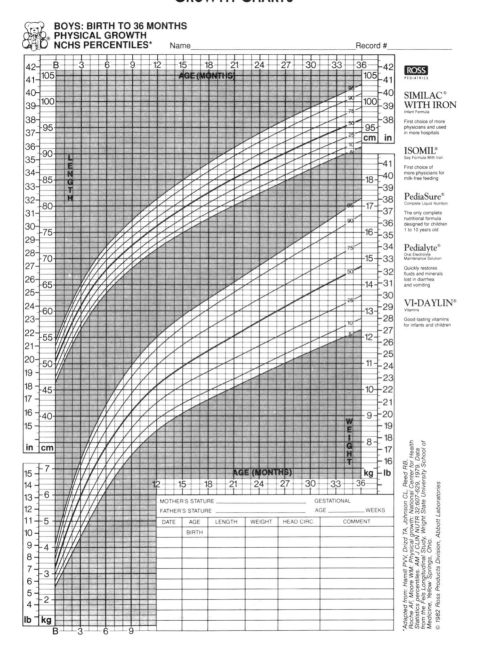

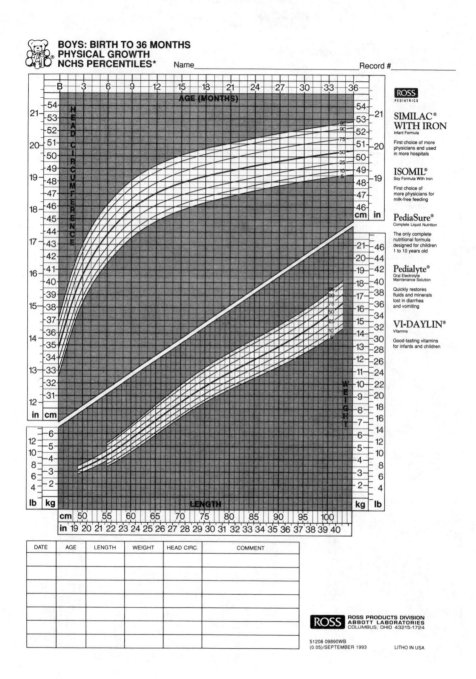

**BOYS: BIRTH TO 36 MONTHS
PHYSICAL GROWTH
NCHS PERCENTILES*** Name_____ Record #_____

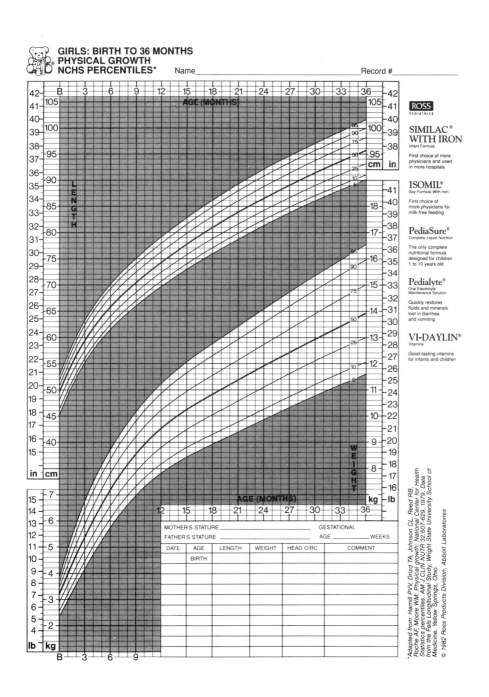

GIRLS: BIRTH TO 36 MONTHS
PHYSICAL GROWTH
NCHS PERCENTILES*

Name_____ Record #_____

ROSS
PEDIATRICS

SIMILAC®
WITH IRON
Infant Formula

First choice of more
physicians and used
in more hospitals

ISOMIL®
Soy Formula With Iron

First choice of
more physicians for
milk-free feeding

PediaSure®
Complete Liquid Nutrition

The only complete
nutritional formula
designed for children
1 to 10 years old

Pedialyte®
Oral Electrolyte
Maintenance Solution

Quickly restores
fluids and minerals
lost in diarrhea
and vomiting

VI-DAYLIN®
Vitamins

Good-tasting vitamins
for infants and children

*Adapted from: Hamill PVV, Drizd TA, Johnson CL, Reed RB,
Roche AF, Moore WM: Physical growth: National Center for Health
Statistics percentiles. AM J CLIN NUTR 32:607-629, 1979. Data
from the Fels Longitudinal Study, Wright State University School of
Medicine, Yellow Springs, Ohio.
© 1982 Ross Products Division, Abbott Laboratories

MOTHER'S STATURE _____ GESTATIONAL
FATHER'S STATURE _____ AGE _____ WEEKS

DATE	AGE	LENGTH	WEIGHT	HEAD CIRC.	COMMENT
	BIRTH				

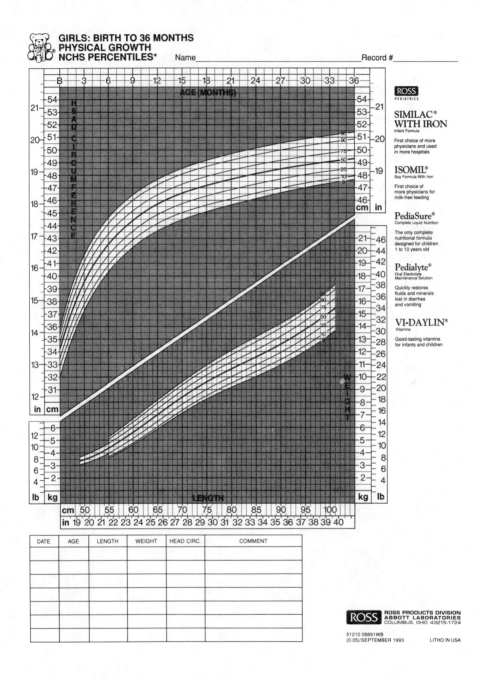

GIRLS: BIRTH TO 36 MONTHS
PHYSICAL GROWTH
NCHS PERCENTILES*   Name_____   Record #_____

DATE	AGE	LENGTH	WEIGHT	HEAD CIRC.	COMMENT

Used with permission of Ross Products Division, Abbott Laboratories, Columbus, Ohio 43216 from NCHS
Growth Charts © 1982 Ross Products Division, Abbott Laboratories

GLOSSARY

Abrasion: An area of the body surface denuded of skin or mucous membrane by some unusual or mechanical process.

Alopecia: Baldness, absence of the hair from skin areas where it normally is present.

Anemia: Any condition in which the number of red blood cells (carriers of oxygen throughout the body) are fewer than normal.

Anorexia: Lack or loss of the appetite for food.

Anorexia nervosa: Prolonged refusal to eat, usually associated with emotional stress. May include binging and purging.

Atrophy: Wasting away of flesh, tissue, cell, or organ.

Avitaminosis: Condition due to complete lack of one or more essential vitamins.

Battered Child Syndrome: A medical condition, primarily of infants and young children, in which there is evidence of *repeated* inflicted injury to the nervous, skin, or skeletal system. Frequently the history as given by the caretaker does not adequately explain the nature of occurrence of the injuries.

Bonding: The psychological attachment of mother to child which develops during and immediately following childbirth. Bonding, which appears to be crucial to the development of a healthy parent/child relationship, may be studied during and immediately following delivery to help identify potential families-at-risk.

Calcification: Formation of bone. The amount of calcium deposited can indicate via X-ray the degree of healing of a broken bone or the location of previous fractures which have healed prior to the X-ray.

Callus: An unorganized meshwork of woven bone, which is formed following fracture of a bone and is normally ultimately replaced by hard adult bone.

Calvarium-(calvaria): Dome-like portion of the skull.

Cataract: An opacity of the crystalline lens of the eye.

Cartilage: The hard connective tissue that is not bone but, in the unborn and growing child, may be the forerunner of bone before calcium is deposited in it.

Cervical: Pertaining to the neck of the cervix (neck-like opening of the uterus).

Clotting factor: Material in the blood that causes it to coagulate. Deficiencies in clotting factors can cause profuse internal or external bleeding and/or bruising, as in the disease hemophilia. Bruises or bleeding caused by such a disease may be mistaken as resulting from abuse.

Coagulation: The process of clotting. The body's process of healing itself when blood is released from an injured vessel.

Coagulation time: The time it takes for blood to coagulate.

Colon: The large intestine.

Comminuted: Broken or crushed into small pieces, as a comminuted fracture.

Concussion: An injury of a soft structure resulting from violent shaking or jarring; usually refers to a brain concussion.

Congenital: Existing at, and usually before birth; referring to conditions that are present at birth, regardless of their causation.

Contusion: A bruise; an injury of a part without a break in the skin.

Cortex: An external layer, as the bark of a tree, or the rind of a fruit. The outer layer of an organ or other body structure, as distinguished from the internal substance.

Cortical: Pertaining to or of the nature of a cortex or bark.

Cortices: Plural of cortex.

Cranium: The skull.

Cutaneous: Pertaining to the skin.

Dehydration: Reduction of water content in the body tissues.

Diaphysis: The shaft of a long bone.

Differential Diagnosis: The determination of which one of two or more diseases or conditions a patient is suffering from by systematically comparing and contrasting their clinical findings.

Dislocation: The displacement of a bone, usually disrupting a joint, which may accompany a fracture or may occur alone.

Distal: Remote; farther from any point of reference; opposed to proximal, (eg., distal fracture of a bone - the end of the bone farthest away from the body trunk).

Duodenum: The first portion of the small intestine connecting the stomach to the jejunum.

Ecchymosis: A small hemorrhagic spot, larger than a petechia, in the skin or mucous membrane forming a nonelevated, round, or irregular blue or purplish patch.

Edema: Swelling caused by an excessive amount of fluid in body tissue. It often follows a bump or bruise but may also be caused by allergy, malnutrition, or disease.

Encopresis: Involuntary passage of feces.

Enuresis: Involuntary passage of urine.

Epiphysis: Growth center near the end of a long bone.

Etiology: Cause of the condition/disease.

Extravasated blood: A discharge or escape of blood from a vessel into the tissues.

Failure to Thrive: (FTT). Growth and developmental failure in presence of considerable familial disturbance with improvement during exposure to a nurturing environment. (Also may be referred to as maltreatment syndrome, rumination syndrome, maternal deprivation, cultural deprivation, emotional deprivation, environmental deprivation, deprivational dwarfism, functional hypopituitarism, growth retardation with maternal deprivation.)

Fetal Alcohol Syndrome: (FAS) A condition in infants resulting from heavy alcohol consumption by the mother during pregnancy. Because alcohol easily crosses the placenta, its concentration in fetal blood equals that in maternal blood. Heavy alcohol intake during pregnancy is associated with numerous adverse effects on the fetus, including mental retardation, hyperactivity, irritability, growth deficiencies, poor suck reflex in infants, and behavioral and learning disabilities. Children with FAS often have distinctive facial characteristics, such as small eyes, short noses, a flat, long upper lip area, and a flattened mid face. Following birth, the infant may suffer from alcohol withdrawal. The incidence of fetal alcohol syndrome in the U.S. is about one in 750 births. Nearly all of these cases involve mothers who drink heavily, meaning more than 45 drinks per month or more than five drinks on any single occasion (Kruse, 1984).

Fomites: Objects, such as clothing, capable of absorbing and transmitting disease.

Frenulum: A fold of mucous membrane which extends from the bottom of the mouth to the bottom of the tongue. Also found in the midline of the upper and lower lips.

Frontal: Referring to the front of the head; the forehead.

Fundoscopic exam: Ophthalmic examination to determine if irregularities or internal injuries to the eye exist.

Genitalia: The external reproductive organs.

Gluteal: Related to the buttocks, which are made up of the large gluteus maximus muscles.

Gram Stain: A laboratory test in which microorganisms are stained with crystal violet.

Growth Hormone: A substance that stimulates growth.

Hematemesis: Vomiting of blood from the stomach, often resulting from internal injuries.

Hematoma: A swelling caused by a collection of blood in an enclosed space, such as under the skin or the skull.

Hematuria: Blood in the urine.

Hemophilia: A hereditary blood clotting disorder characterized by spontaneous or traumatic internal and external bleeding and bruising.

Hemorrhage: The escape of blood from vessels; bleeding. Small hemorrhages are classified according to size as petechia (very small), purpura (up to 1 cm.) and ecchymosis (larger).

Hyperactive: More active than is considered normal.

Hyperthermia: Condition of high body temperature.

Hyphema: Suffused with blood, blood-shot, especially of the eyes. Hemorrhage within the anterior chamber of the eye.

Hyperkinesis: Excessive motion or activity (also called hyperactivity).

Hyperpigmentation: Increased pigmentation (coloring) of the skin.

Hypoactive: Less active than is considered normal.

Hypoglycemia: An abnormally diminished content of glucose in the blood which may lead to tremulousness, cold sweat, hypothermia, headache, accompanied by confusion, hallucinations, bizarre behavior, and ultimately convulsions and coma.

Hypopigmentation: Abnormally diminished pigmentation, as distinct from complete loss of pigment.

Hypothalamus: The portion of the brain which controls and integrates many functions such as general regulation of water balance, body temperature, sleep, food intake, and the development of secondary sex characteristics.

Hypothermia: Low body temperature, usually secondary to prolonged exposure to cold.

Ileum: Final portion of the small intestine which connects the colon.

Impetigo: A highly contagious, rapidly spreading skin disorder which occurs principally in infants and young children. The disease, characterized by red blisters, may be an indicator of neglect and poor living conditions.

Intraocular: Within the eye.

Jejunum: The midportion of the small intestine which extends from the duodenum to the ileum.

Laceration: A cut.

Lateral: Toward the side.

Lesion: Any injury to any part of the body from any cause that results in damage or loss of structure or function of the body tissue involved. A lesion may be caused by poison, infection, dysfunction, or violence, and may be either accidental or intentional.

Long Bone: General term applied to the bones of the leg or the arm.

Lumbar: Pertaining to the loins, the part of the back between the thorax and the pelvis.

Malnutrition: Faulty intake of food and drink requirements necessary for maintenance, growth, activity, reproduction, and lactation. Results from malassimilation or poor diet.

Mandible: The bone of the lower jaw.

Marasmus: A form of protein-calorie malnutrition chiefly occurring during the first year of life, characterized by growth retardation and progressive wasting of subcutaneous fat and muscle, but usually with the retention of appetite and mental alertness.

Medial: Toward the middle or midline.

Menkes Kinky Hair Syndrome: Rare, inherited disease resulting in brittle bones and, eventually, death. It is found in infants and, because of the great number of fractures the child may exhibit, can be mistaken for child abuse.

Mesentery: A membranous fold attaching various organs to the body wall.

Metabolism: The sum of all the physical and chemical processes by which living organized substance is produced and maintained; the transformation by which energy is made available for the uses of the organism.

Metaphysis: The wider part of the long bone between the end and the shaft.

Mongolian spots: A type of birthmark that can appear anywhere on a child's body, most frequently on the lower back. These dark spots usually fade by age five. They can be mistaken for bruises.

Occipital: Referring to the back of the head.

Ossification: The formation of bone or bony substance.

Osteogenesis Imperfecta: An inherited condition in which the bones are abnormally brittle and subject to fractures.

Osteomyelitis: Inflammation of bone caused by a bacterial organism.

Pathognomonic: Specifically distinctive or characteristic of a disease or pathologic condition; a sign or symptom on which a diagnosis can be made.

Perinatal: Around the time of birth, both immediately before and afterward.

Perineum: The space between the anus and the scrotum or vagina.

Periosteum: A specialized connective tissue covering all bones of the body, and possessing bone-forming potentialities.

Peritoneum: The lining of the abdomen.

Peritonitis: Inflammation of the peritoneum secondary to infection or trauma.

Petechia: A small, pinpoint, nonraised, perfectly round, purplish red spot caused by intradermal or submucous hemorrhage, which later turns blue or yellow.

Polyphagia: Excessive or voracious eating.

Proximal: Nearest; closer to any point of reference; opposed to distal. (eg., the end of a bone closest to the body trunk).

Radiolucent: Permitting the passage of X-rays without leaving a shadow on the film. Soft tissues are radiolucent; bones are not.

Recurrent Otitis Media: Repeated inflammation of the middle ear. A leading cause of hearing loss in children.

Retina: Inside lining of the eye. Injury to the head can cause bleeding or detachment of the retina, possibly causing blindness.

Retinal hemorrhage: A finding frequently associated with shaking or head trauma.

Revascularization: The process of again becoming vascular, or the natural or surgically induced development of vessels in the tissue.

Rickets: A condition caused by deficiency of vitamin D, especially in infancy and childhood, with disturbance of normal development of bones.

Sacral area: Lower part of the back.

Scalded Skin Syndrome (Staphylococcal) (SSS): This is a severe bacterial infection that causes large blisters and redness of the skin. This is not caused by a burn and blisters occur all over the body including inside the mouth.

Scapula: The flat, triangular bone in the back of the shoulder; the shoulder blade.

Sclera: The tough white outer layer of the eyeball, covering approximately the posterior five-sixths of its surface.

Scurvy: A condition due to deficiency of ascorbic acid (vitamin C) in the diet and marked by weakness, anemia, spongy gums, and other symptoms.

Secondary Infection: Infection by a microorganism following an infection by another kind of microorganism.

Seizures: Uncontrollable muscular contractions, usually alternating with muscular relaxation and generally accompanied by unconsciousness. Seizures, which vary in intensity and length of occurrence, are the result of some brain irritation which has been caused by disease, inherited condition, fever, tumor, vitamin deficiency, or injury to the head.

Serology: The study of blood serum for evidence of infection.

Skeletal survey: A series of X-rays that studies all bones of the body. Such a survey should be done in all cases of suspected abuse to locate any old, as well as new, fractures which may exist.

"Slapped Cheek" Disease (Fifth's Disease): A viral infection which has a unique facial rash characterized by bright red cheeks. The cheeks are diffusely red as if they had just been slapped. This is not caused by abuse and finger markings and bruises will not be present.

Subarachnoidal space: The innermost of the three membranes covering the brain and spinal cord. A site of hemorrhage.

Subconjunctival: Situated or occurring beneath the conjunctiva. (The delicate membrane that lines the eyelids and covers the eyeball). A site of hemorrhage.

Subcutaneous: Beneath the skin.

Subdural hematoma: A common symptom of abused children, consisting of a collection of blood beneath the outermost membrane covering the brain and spinal cord. The hematoma may be caused by a blow to the head or from shaking a baby or small child. (See also WHIPLASH SHAKEN INFANT SYNDROME).

Subgaleal: The inner lining of the scalp; a site of hemorrhage frequently secondary to hair pulling.

Sudden Infant Death Syndrome (SIDS): Sudden Infant Death Syndrome is the sudden, unexpected death of any infant in whom a thorough postmortem examination fails to demonstrate a clear cause of death. Several recent studies suggest that some infant deaths attributed to SIDS were, when investigated further, found to be related to other previously unknown causes, most commonly suffocation by a caretaker.

Sutures: A type of fibrous joint in which the opposed surfaces are closely united, as in the skull.

Temporal: Referring to the side of the head.

Trabecula: A general term for a supporting or anchoring strand of tissue.

Trauma: An internal or external injury or wound brought about by an outside force. Usually trauma means injury by violence, but it may also apply to the wound caused by any surgical procedure. Trauma may be caused accidentally or, as in a case of physical abuse, nonaccidentally. Trauma is also a term applied to physiological discomfort or symptoms resulting from an emotional shock or painful experience.

Turgor: Condition of being swollen and congested. This can refer to normal or other fullness.

Vascular: Of the blood vessels.

Whiplash Shaken Infant Syndrome: The violent shaking, throwing or twirling of an infant or child causing massive traumatic intracranial and intraocular (eye) bleedings. Often linked with brain damage and mental retardation.

REFERENCES

Dorland's Illustrated Medical Dictionary. (24th ed.) New York, W.B. Saunders Co., 1965.

Midwest Parent-Child Welfare Resource Center. (1977). *Interdisciplinary glossary.* Milwaukee, WI: School of Social Welfare, University of Wisconsin-Milwaukee.

About AHA

The American Humane Association (AHA), a nonprofit corporation headquartered in Englewood, Colorado, is the nation's oldest agency dedicated to the protection of children from abuse and neglect. Since 1878, AHA, through its Children's Division, has provided national leadership in the development of programs, policies, and services on behalf of children who are abused and neglected.

AHA's main objectives are to: 1) increase the abilities, knowledge and effectiveness of child welfare professionals and child welfare agencies; 2) enhance the community's capacity to respond effectively to the needs of vulnerable children and families; 3) improve the information and capacities available to public and voluntary child welfare agencies that help them respond effectively to child abuse and neglect; and 4) facilitate a concerted national response to the problem of child maltreatment.

As a national association of child protection programs, agencies, and individuals, AHA's membership includes state and local social service agencies, courts, hospitals, schools, mental health professionals, professional social workers, child advocates, and concerned individuals in every state. AHA provides professionals and concerned citizens with facts, resources, and referrals they need to make informed decisions to help children and families in crisis. AHA is guided by a national program advisory committee and by a national Board of Directors.

With a comprehensive set of staff capabilities, AHA works in an array of areas to improve all aspects of child welfare system operations. AHA accomplishes its work through:

- Convening ongoing national forums to address cutting-edge issues in child welfare (such as outcome measures and risk assessment);

- Designing and facilitating training efforts in partnership with state and local child welfare agencies;

- Conducting program evaluation and research processes which help child welfare agencies improve service delivery;

- Providing national and state-specific technical assistance on data collection and utilization; and

- Publishing resources which help professionals, agencies and communities better meet the needs of vulnerable children and their families.

AHA is further committed to developing resources and programs to help communities and individual citizens take positive steps toward preventing child abuse in their own neighborhoods. Assistance is needed in building a more responsive system that includes community participation. With our legacy-based foundation of involvement and expertise, AHA intends to remain at the forefront of protecting abused and neglected children long into the next century.